ST. GEORGE
AND THE
DRAGON

AND
THE QUEST
FOR THE
HOLY GRAIL

ST. GEORGE
AND THE
DRAGON
AND
THE QUEST
FOR THE
HOLY GRAIL

WRITTEN AND ILLUMINATED
BY
EDWARD HAYS

Forest of Peace Books, Inc.

OTHER BOOKS BY THE AUTHOR:
(available from Forest of Peace Books, Inc.)

The Magic Lantern
In Pursuit of the Great White Rabbit
Prayers for a Planetary Pilgrim
A Pilgrim's Almanac
Prayers for the Domestic Church
Prayers for the Servants of God
Secular Sanctity
Twelve and One-Half Keys
Sundancer
The Ethiopian Tattoo Shop
Pray All Ways

Forest of Peace Books, Inc.

ST. GEORGE AND THE DRAGON
AND THE QUEST FOR THE HOLY GRAIL

copyright © 1986, by Edward M. Hays

Library of Congress Catalog Card Number: 85-82568
ISBN 0-939516-07-1

published by
Forest of Peace Books, Inc.
P.O. Box 269
Leavenworth, Kansas 66048-0269 U.S.A.

printed by
Hall Directory, Inc.
Topeka, Kansas 66608

first printing: March 1986
second printing: February 1987
third printing: May 1988
fourth printing: September 1989
fifth printing: October 1990
sixth printing: July 1991
seventh printing: May 1992

cover design by
Edward Hays

calligraphy by
Thomas Turkle

Written and Published during the
Return of Halley's Comet, 1985-86 A.D.

The illustration above is a copy of an artist's image of Halley's
Comet as it appeared in April of 1066. The design is from
the 11th century Bayeux Tapestry with the inscription "In-
stimirant Stella" flowing out behind the comet – "These men
wonder at the star." May wonder still be alive when in 2160
Halley's Comet visits our planet again.

Dedicated

to my friend

Gregory Bien

e footsteps on gallant knight
h for the life-giving vessel-

FROM ONE OF THE BOOKS IN THE ATTIC. AH!!! THE ADVENTURE OF IT ALL!

IMPORTANT:
A NOTE TO THE READER

The book you are about to read is a journal written by a man named George. No last name was given in the original manuscript, but the title "St."appears before the name at the beginning of the log.

This is apparently a report of certain events and reflections recorded in a garage-hermitage located behind George's home. The journal was originally. written in longhand and has been transcribed as faithfully as possible in this book.

Also, while the day of the week and the month were noted, the year was not recorded. Therefore, the precise date of these most unusual events can only be approximated.

We have also duplicated drawings found here and there in the journal. We can only surmise that they are also George's. Since they are related to his notes, we have included them in this book.

We regret to say that we are not at liberty to disclose how we came to possess this unique diary. May these pages be as fascinating to you as they were to us.

Saturday, March 15th

I begin my journal just after dawn on this Saturday before the Spring Equinox. I wish to record the events that led up to this date and to the use of part of my garage as a hermitage. My story began several weeks ago when I began to feel an unexplainable urge to set out on a spiritual journey.

I felt it deep within myself — the call to go on a holy quest. Now such a calling would have been understandable in the Middle Ages, but this is the end of the twentieth century! My wife was outraged that she should be expected to stay home, care for the children and pay the bills while I trooped off to strange and distant lands! My boss thought that I was suffering from burn-out and suggested therapy, while my neighbors only shook their heads in disbelief. Even the travel agent to whom I had gone was bewildered by my request. "I'm sorry," she said, "we don't have any brochures or information on 'lands of quest.' "

But I — non-hero, ordinary middle-class fellow — heard the call. In the attic of my house I found my great-grandfather's rusty army sword. Packing a few personal items, I bade farewell to my angry wife, confused children and chuckling neighbors and left home, my sword sheathed at my side.

I walked all that day and into the night. As the stars came out, I saw the constellation of Draco, high in the northern sky. For some unknown reason this large, curved sweep of stars gave me a sense of hope. As I walked along, I kept looking up at it for guidance. But with each step it became more and more difficult to keep my eyes on the stars, for the branches overhead grew denser and denser. They wove themselves into such a covered canopy that it became pitch dark — as black as the soul of a witch. I began to wonder if I had lost my way.

Suddenly, with an explosion of energy, sparkling lights and balls of scarlet fire, an enormous dragon stood before me! Its serpent-like body was covered with scarlet scales that flashed orange and yellow. The tail of the dragon was barbed with spear-like points, and it was huge! Smoke and flames poured out of its wide mouth, lined with great white teeth. I was terrified. I dropped my sword and fell to my knees. But then, coming to my senses, I jumped to my feet and turned to run. Suddenly, however, I stopped short and said aloud, "Wait — a dragon, a real live dragon! It's only natural that I should meet a dragon if I'm on a quest. Wonderful! Meeting one face to face on my very first night is a clear sign that I'm on the right path." As my knees rattled together, I continued, "But I wish I weren't so frightened." Closing my eyes, I picked up my sword and marched right toward the flame-spitting, scarlet-scaled dragon.

"Hello, stranger. You look like you're lost. Can I be of any assistance?" asked the dragon in a voice tinged with tiredness.

I stopped dead in my tracks, lowered my sword and said, "Well, er . . . yes, I am lost, I must confess. But I am on a quest, you see, and from all I have read it seems that people who are on quests are frequently lost."

"That's correct," agreed the dragon. "Those who know where they're going in life usually aren't going anywhere, at least anywhere important. But you say you are on a quest? What are you seeking?"

"I'm not sure — the Voice never said. Perhaps Truth, Freedom, the Holy Grail, the Fountain of Youth, Eternal Life or . . . ," and swallowing with difficulty, I added, "to Kill the Dragon." At these words the dragon only yawned, sending a great

10

orange-red fireball crackling through the cool, damp night air.

"Excuse me," said the dragon, "but it's been a long day and not an easy one. Contrary to all that you have read, my friend, dragons are not all bad, all evil. My days are spent aiding travelers lost in the forest, caring for the needs of the poor who live in the mountains and doing other kind deeds in out-of-the-way places. The old map makers were right when they drew us dragons on the charts where nothing existed. My work is hard, but I find it rewarding. My life has lots of pains, but I suffer them gladly."

I remembered what I had once read about dragons, how they are clever and cunning. Their very name means "sharp-sighted"; like serpents, they are said to be diabolically clever. Maybe this old dragon was tricking me, leading me on, only to destroy me in one fiery blast.

"Do you have a name?" asked the dragon, looking me straight in the eye.

"Well, yes, I'm called George," I replied.

"George? Is that all, just plain George?" asked the dragon. "Nothing in front of it, like Saint George or Sir George? How can you expect to be treated with proper respect as one on a quest if you have no title? Who will believe you if you are just plain George?"

"Well, perhaps you're right, Dragon," I replied. "My neighbors think I'm mad, my boss thinks I'm suffering from burn-out and my wife, I am sure, thinks I'm having an affair. But all that's ever in front of my name are the two letters 'MR.' "

"Sorry, George," replied the dragon. "They won't do; no romance in 'MR.' — or color either. We will have to give you a proper title if you wish to go on a quest." With a dramatic flourish the dragon drew himself up to full height and announced in a deep, regal voice, "I, the Celestial Dragon, dub thee with the title of 'ST.' You may have it printed on your laun-

dry tags for your socks and underwear and have it painted on your mailbox — hence to be known by that title to everyone."

"With all due respect, Dragon, you can't do that. Only the Pope can make someone a saint."

" 'ST.,' my dear quester," said the dragon, "doesn't mean 'Saint'; it is the abbreviation of the four-letter word 'Sent.' You, my friend, are George-who-is-sent, or Sent George. You have to be sent before you can become a saint. And it seems that the Voice is calling you or sending you on your quest."

"Thank you, thank you so much," I said. "That is most kind of you. I've always thought of dragons as evil, but I apologize for thinking that about you."

"I am a Chinese dragon," said the old dragon. "There's a difference, you know! In China and the East, dragons are a good sign, one of blessing and good fortune. And I come from the line of dragons that is the symbol of the royal family — see, I even have five claws, while an ordinary Chinese dragon has only four! Historically, however, we do have a bad name. Heroes like Hercules, Siegfried, Beowulf, King Arthur and even your patron, St. George, were all dragon slayers. It's because we have bodies similar to serpents that we are considered evil. Dr. Freud would have a heyday with that fear. Indeed, all who set out on a quest go looking for a dragon or some ugly, fierce monster to kill, but the real enemies are not outside forces in some dark forest — but rather, they are inside."

Although the dragon made good sense, I was growing tired. It had been a long and difficult day, and I had to move on. The dragon smiled and said to me, "Everyone on a quest needs a good companion, a faithful and trusted guide. Let me be yours; I know this forest well. Come, climb up on my back," said the dragon as he made a great deep bow with his scaly neck and head.

Now it didn't make book sense, but I found myself liking this tired old dragon with his scarlet scales and great five-clawed feet. I felt like a prince as I rode on the back of the dragon. From this position high on his humped back, I noticed that the dragon's body was covered with old wounds. Whenever the dragon breathed forth fire to light the path in front of us, I noticed that the wounds glowed golden-red in the dark. I also noticed how the dragon limped now and then, but as it was the end of the day, I thought that he might just be tired. The old wounds did, however, arouse my curiosity, and when I asked about them, the dragon replied, "Oh, my friend, I have been slain a thousand times, but I have always arisen again. These old wounds are the source of my power and my insight. As I said, our greatest and worst enemies are not the monsters who roam the forest or even wicked witches or evil wizards. No, it is our scars, our wounds and old injuries that we must fear. As we journey through life we all have been injured — hurt by parents, brothers or sisters, schoolmates, strangers, lovers, teachers . . . the possible list of the guilty is long. Each wound has the power to talk to us, you know. They speak, however, with crooked voices because of the scars. But allow me to tell you a story that will make my point clear." I was so caught up in the words of my dragon companion that I forgot my own weariness.

"Once upon a time," began the dragon, "a great samurai warrior with two great swords hanging from his belt approached a monk and said, 'Tell me, holy monk, about heaven and hell.' The orange-robed monk looked up at the warrior from where he sat and replied in a quiet voice, 'I cannot tell you about heaven and hell because you are much too stupid.' The samurai warrior was filled with rage. He clenched his fists and gave a fierce shout as he reached for one of his swords. 'Besides that you are

very ugly,' added the monk. The samurai's eyes flamed and his heart was incensed as he drew his sword. 'That,' said the little monk, 'is hell.' Struck by the power of the words and the wisdom of this teaching, the warrior dropped his sword, bowed his head and sank to his knees. 'And that,' said the monk, 'is heaven.'

"You see," continued the dragon, "the words of the monk touched old wounds, perhaps wounds that were made when the warrior was a child and was called stupid, dumb or ugly. It was his wounds that caused hell to capture him. All of us have wounds — old ones and new ones — and whenever the monster appears, when hell breaks loose, we know that our old wounds are talking, guiding us. It is these wounds that must be confronted and not us poor, innocent dragons."

"But," I said, "your wounds glow with great beauty, and you said they are the source of your power and magic. How can my wounds become a source of power?"

"First," replied the dragon, "you must not give in to the voice of your scars, the voice of the times you trusted and were betrayed, loved and were rejected, did your best and were laughed at. Do not give weight to the scars left because you were slighted or were made to feel less than others. Instead, when those voices call to you to react with envious or jealous feelings, do exactly the opposite. When they say, 'run away,' you must stay. When they whisper, 'distance yourself,' then come all the closer. You must transform their power, not destroy it! That, my friend, is really being involved in a quest. All quests begin with some question. Great quests begin, naturally, with great questions. 'Why am I not happy?' 'Why am I not a saint?' 'How do I find happiness?' That's what you're questing for, George — happiness. And happiness, health, holiness and all

14

the rest come only when we have made our injuries into glorious wounds."

I felt a surge of excitement. Indeed, it was a great adventure to be on a quest.

The old Chinese dragon with the wounds that glowed so beautifully in the dark was indeed wise. I saw how my behavior, which had so often hurt myself and others, had flowed from the fact that I had listened to the voice of some old wound. I realized what the dragon was saying to me. Yes, I must learn to listen to my pain as well as my pleasures. And I need to distinguish between the different voices I hear within myself, the voices of old wounds and the small quiet voice that comes from somewhere deep inside. It is this quiet voice that calls me to sacrifice, to generosity and to kindness, but it frequently has been outshouted by the angry voices of my wounds. I have to begin a friendship with myself, with all of myself. Perhaps the goodness that I have been seeking on my quest is really all inside me.

And, suddenly, there we were, standing on the edge of the forest. Off to the east, the first light of dawn was on the horizon. I was amazed because we had stopped directly behind my own home. There was my back yard, my garage, the patio with the outdoor grill. And warm, yellow light filled the kitchen windows. I felt my heart sink, and I asked, "Is my quest over? Must I return so soon to my family, my work and daily duties?"

"Yes and no," replied the old dragon. "You have heard the Voice; you have been sent upon a great adventure. This is only the beginning, I promise you. If you wish, you and I together will visit strange and distant places; we shall unlock ancient secrets. But now, George, it's time for breakfast — I can smell the coffee brewing. Go home, George, and remember you are sent. You are sent to heal yourself, your fami-

ly and the world with your wounds." And with that
the great old dragon leaned over and, kissing me,
enveloped me in a cloud of flaming breath.

Noon

Pause to eat a small lunch of bread, cheese and fruit.

Once again I take up the events that have led up
to this day. After the dragon had disappeared, I stood
outside my back door, dreading to open it. Only
having been away overnight, I was too embarrassed
to return. Inside the kitchen I could hear the voices
of my children gathered around the breakfast table.
The television was on with the morning news. I
opened the door, and Martha, my wife, said, "Well,
kids, look who's at our door: Sir Lancelot has come
home again after an all-night meeting of the Round
Table!" Without asking, she handed me a cup of
coffee and said, "What happened, George, did Lady
Guinevere turn into a dragon at dawn?"

"No," I replied, "I just felt that I should come back
(I lied). Be patient, Martha, I'm trying to work
through something. I just need time, please."

The children were confused, and the oldest was
ready to ask a question when Martha said, "Time for
school, up and at 'em!"

I returned to work that morning and swallowed
my pride for a second time as I was greeted with the
jokes of my fellow workers. All day long I could not
forget the dragon I had met the night before. I hope
that some day these wounds to my pride will glow
as his did. That day they did not shine, they only
stung. When I returned home, I realized that I
needed time to think, and more than time I needed
a quiet place. At home, every room is crammed with
confusion and noise. The television is always on, even
when no one is watching. The appliances take turns,

16

it seems, in deafening duets of racket. The kids seem to be continuously arguing, and that teenager next door plays his stereo as if he had a friend in Africa who wants to listen.

In pure desperation I went to the garage and sat in the car. Secretly I wished that I could be exiled to the most remote region of Siberia. Then the idea hit me: this is my Siberia. The garage is at the farthest limits of my property, and behind the garage is an old tool shed that's used mostly for storage. My mind raced ahead with the plans. I would clean up and repair the old tool shed behind the garage and make it into a hermitage where I might find some quiet space. I need that quiet or I'll go mad — as if I weren't already. Have I really seen a dragon?

MAY I ALSO GO IN SEARCH OF THE HOLY GRAIL

"There never was a human so ill but that if one day he sees the Holy Grail he cannot die within the week, that follows . . . his appearance will stay the same as on the day . . . sees it . . . and it will never change, save that his hair might turn gray." from von Eschenbach's "Parzival"

17

Saturday, March 22nd

For the last several evenings after supper, I've been coming out here to clean up the shed, doing some minor repairs. Now I have a hermitage that has all the possibilities of Thoreau's cabin, even if it lacks the woods.

Today, as I spend my first full day here, I am not sure what is supposed to happen in a hermitage. But like the call to the quest, I felt compelled to build it and to come to it on a regular basis. Secretly, if I am honest, I guess I hope that the dragon will return. Maybe this converted tool shed is nothing more than a rendezvous point, a waiting room. May this log which I have begun today be a record of what I dream and hope will happen.

10:30 A.m.

I begin again after a short time of trying to be quiet. The silence feels good, but my head is full of racket. I wonder how to turn it off. Questions keep knocking at my door: Am I really going crazy? Am I being deluded by the idea of a quest? What do I hope to gain by it all? Maybe I should listen to my wife and neighbors and "come to my senses," being content with the "good" life I have. Why can't I be like other people and be satisfied with the usual after-work activities − golf, fishing or some hobby?

11:00 A.m

I was shocked and delighted by the appearance of a visitor at my door. It was the dragon! He asked if he could come in, which he did without waiting for a reply. While the shed is small, he accommodated himself to it rather well. With a smile that exposed all of his white, pointed teeth, he said, "So you're having second thoughts about going on a quest? Well, George, that's not at all uncommon: leaving a comfortable life and familiar habits isn't an easy decision to make. The reality of taking up a quest always leads to serious questions. But let them all go for a moment, and let me tell you a story about some others who had a choice to make.

Once upon a time there was a great prison. Its tall grey walls of massive concrete, its numerous guard towers and complete absence of windows only confirmed the fact that it was indeed a maximum security prison. The prison had an unsoiled reputation, for no prisoner had ever escaped alive.

But nothing challenges the human spirit like the impossible, and a small gang of prisoners had been working for a long time to dig an escape tunnel under the prison walls. The idea was ingenious: the entrance to the tunnel was under the bathtub in the shower room, and the dirt could be removed, one small pail at a time, and washed down the shower drains.

The gang called themselves the Escape Committee, and their leader was a man named Jack. His conviction that no prison is escape-proof, his electric sense of hope and promise and his belief in the impossible had fired the little gang with enthusiasm. They labored for months on their secret tunnel until Jack announced that, by his calculations, they were beyond the walls. On the day for the escape, they gathered at the entrance of the dark and narrow tunnel. Jack could see the fear in their eyes.

"I'll go first. Wait here and if I find any trouble I'll come back to warn you. If I'm not back in three

19

hours, you'll know it's safe to follow me." Then, turning to a muscular, tough-looking member of the gang, Jack said, "And you, Rocky, are the new leader of the Escape Committee. Make sure that everyone gets out!" And with a nod Jack disappeared down the dark tunnel.

They waited as they had been told. When Jack did not return, they began preparations for their escape, jubilant with excitement. Rocky did a test run of the escape tunnel; when he found it safe, he returned to the entrance. With his strong arms he slid aside the bathtub and began to climb out of the hole — into a circle of armed guards!

"Get out of there," snapped the chief warden. "You fools — don't you know this is an escape-proof prison? No one gets out of here!"

As they handcuffed him, Rocky said, "Jack escaped — he got away!"

"I'll have you know," replied the warden, "that we have guarded the path of this stupid tunnel for weeks. And I guarantee you that no one has come out the other end. Now follow me." The warden and the guards led Rocky out of the shower room and up to the top floor of the prison to the warden's office and living quarters.

The warden stood at his desk and fingered through a manila file. "Number 353549 — 'Rocky' I believe they call you in the cell blocks — I find your behavior foolish. You're lucky you're alive. We must not allow this attempted escape to go unpunished, for that would set a bad example. Yet I have something I want to show you." The warden walked over to a set of large windows on one wall and drew back the heavy green drapes. "Come here and look below." Rocky saw the prison yard filled with prisoners dressed in the same grey uniforms, staring lifelessly at the ground. The warden said, "Take a good look at them. Even if you and your gang did escape, what about all these poor creatures? They have no hope, nothing to dream about. What about them, Number 353549?

"And what's outside these walls? Who knows if there's more freedom than both prisoners and guards have in here? This prison needs something unique — and you, Number 353549, are just the person with the power to create it. What this prison needs is an 'official' Escape Committee!"

Dumbfounded, Rocky stared at the warden. At that moment a prison guard wheeled in a dinner cart loaded with fine wines, heaping plates of roast beef and other rich food. He was followed by another guard who rolled in a beautifully set table for two, complete with lighted candles. "Come," said the warden, "we can talk about it over dinner. I'm starved."

And so, night after night, Rocky was taken from his cell in solitary confinement to have dinner with the warden. The other prisoners, believing he was being taken for torture, shuddered as he was marched past their cells. Rocky slowly grew to understand the plan the warden proposed. Hope could come to those hopeless ones sentenced to life in prison; all they needed was an Escape Committee. Then they could dream of freedom outside the grey walls of the prison.

So Rocky organized countless committees, all under the leadership of the Escape Committee. At their weekly meetings plans were drawn up for the great escape. The story of Jack was told and retold, saying that he had escaped to freedom! The symbol of the Escape Committee was an upright shovel with the sun behind it. It was a secret sign, yet everyone possessed one. Soon, even some of the guards became members. Like the rising of the sun, hope gradually began to appear in the prison. Singing, once never heard within its walls, became common. Flower gardens appeared in the prison yard and the entire environment began to change. Once when the warden was sick with the flu for a week, he entrusted the ongoing maintenance of the prison to his friend Rocky, who had a wonderful organizational skill. In fact, the warden was able to take frequent vacations from his office, confident that Rocky would keep everything in order.

Now, even though the main work of the Escape Committee and its vast network of sub-committees was escape, no one ever escaped! Even when those who were initiated into this secret organization were taken to the shower room and shown the tunnel, no one ever attempted to use it! In fact, once or twice when someone actually suggested using it, the Escape Committee denounced them. They were isolated from all social contact with the other prisoners by a most painful form of solitary confinement: they were not placed in some dark cell but were allowed to remain as part of the population of the prison. However, they were never spoken to, touched or looked at. So great was the effect of this punishment that after a few attempts no one even raised the question of escaping.

The warden's ingenious plan made life inside the prison better for everyone. He and the guards did not have to worry about anyone escaping; life and work inside the prison went on without trouble. The leaders of the Escape Committee were given special cells and had their own excellent dining room. They were also shown respect by both guards and fellow prisoners. And the prisoners, once clouded by despair, now lived with a sense of hope and promise. Their meager, imprisoned lives now had meaning. The arrangement was, shall we say, "perfect!"

This story ends as all good stories end . . . "They lived happily ever after . . . ."

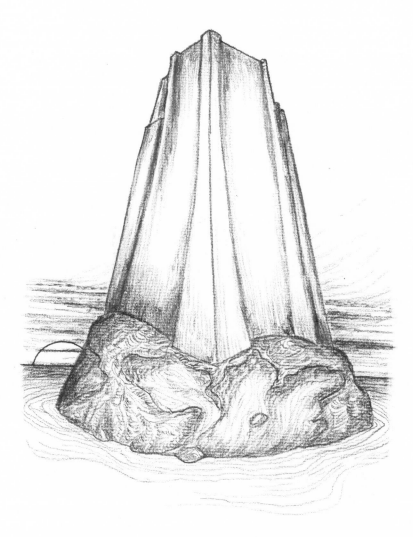

We sat in silence for a moment after he had finished the story. Then I began by saying, "That doesn't sound like a happy ending to me: they were all still in prison!"

"Yes, George, but how many people do you know who settle for something less than freedom? How many content themselves with a few luxuries and the sense of being part of a group? But I can see in your face that despite your doubts you are not satisfied with life as it has been. You are worried that you can't lose yourself in the pursuits that other people find so rewarding." I nodded in agreement, awed that the dragon knew even my most private thoughts. "If you have time to listen," he continued, "I have another story to tell you about a man who also faced a choice. Sit back, then, close your eyes and let the magic theater inside your head begin as I tell you about Joe Moss.

Joe Moss was not a religious man, yet his ears rang with an echo of the gospel he had heard that morning in church! Back and forth the words ricocheted, as if his head were some great canyon. It was no ordinary echo that grows fainter with repetition; this echo grew louder as it persisted in his head: " YOU WILL KNOW THAT HE IS NEAR, STANDING AT YOUR DOOR."

Now, as I said, Joe Moss was not a religious man. His relationship with God, Church and prayer was like that of many persons — it was mainly a spectator sport. Joe related to Church as he did to baseball; he was not actively or personally involved but was an observer of the skills of others. Joe admired those who worshipped with deep reverence but felt no such call to holiness or prayer within himself. So this strange religious experience, the haunting declaration of the nearness

24

of Jesus Christ, was *most* unsettling.

For seven days and nights the echo continued. Perplexed and disturbed, Joe went to visit his pastor. "Ah, yes," the pastor explained, "you are speaking about the glorious Second Coming, or as we say in Greek, the Parousia! The early Church believed it to be near at hand, following upon a great world catastrophe. 2 Peter, chapter 3, verse 10: 'The day of the Lord will come like a thief .... On that day ... the heavens will vanish with a roar: the earth ... destroyed by fire ....' " Without even a pause to catch his breath, the pastor poured out an endless stream of scholarly speculation on the theology of the Second Coming. More confused than before, Joe excused himself and left the pastor midstream in his monologue —carrying with him, unanswered, the question he had come with: "Why am I, Joe Moss, suffering from this relentless religious echo?"

After a round robin of visits to clergy, psychologists and even an ear specialist, Joe finally settled on a suggestion made by a plumber who had come to fix his leaky toilet. Joe stood in his bathroom, watching the plumber work. In that most intimate room which possesses the same magic as a confessional, Joe told the plumber of his strange problem. With far more insight than any of the other repairmen of society Joe had visited, the plumber advised: "Don't fight it. What you resist, persists! Just let it wear itself out. Spend three days in solitude, eat nothing and drink lots of water. If the pain continues, see your family physician."

The plumber's prescription was right. At the end of the third day of solitude the echo began to subside, growing fainter and fainter. By 11:30 that night it had disappeared completely. Joe was over-joyed — and hungry — since he had fasted for three days. Without turning on the light, he entered the darkened kitchen and opened the refrigerator door. A pie-shaped beam of white light stabbed the darkness as if a lighthouse had suddenly switched on its beacon. On the bright shelves inside, Joe could see an array of heavenly delights: sliced ham, cheese, a loaf of brown bread, a jar of mayonnaise and chilled beer. But before he could reach for any of these, he saw at the edge of the opened door a non-human figure that froze him in his tracks. "YOU WILL KNOW THAT HE IS NEAR," spoke the figure, "YES, STANDING AT YOUR DOOR."

Joe was filled with dismay. He grabbed for words like a drowning man reaching for a life preserver in a shipwreck. "Who are you? I . . . I . . . It's impossible!"

While part of his mind was helplessly stuck between neutral and first gear, another part raced ahead: "Am I hallucinating? Is this the result of too much fasting?"

The mysterious figure at the opened refrigerator door smiled and spoke as if the center of Joe's forehead were a large picture window, "No, Joseph, you are not hallucinating. It is I. Do not be afraid, for I come with good news: I come to call you to life everlasting." Joe sank to his knees on the kitchen floor in the center of that shaft of brilliant light that streamed from his refrigerator. A delightfully cool breeze flowed over the top of the mayonnaise jar, down across the sliced ham and out into the kitchen. The coolness felt good, for Joe's forehead was wet with sweat. "I'm not a religious man," Joe blurted out. "Why me? And I never thought you would look like this! I do remember hearing that when the Lord would come to my door, it would be like a thief in the night. But I never thought you would come

26

through my refrigerator door! And certainly not as a *cockroach*!"

"That's right, Joe; 'You don't know the exact day or the hour — or how the Lord will come,' " replied the huge black cockroach with a laugh that rang through the house. "I am the Lord of Life, and those who follow me shall live forever." As he spoke, he reached over and swung the refrigerator door shut. "We're wasting a lot of energy with that door standing open. And I prefer the moonlight coming in through the kitchen window to that glaring refrigerator light."

For a second time, Joe was surprised. He had always imagined that if he ever had a vision of Jesus, everything would be surrounded with heavenly golden light. Yet the Lord seemed more at home in the darkness. Realizing that his every thought was being read, Joe tried to block out his disgust at the Lord's repulsive appearance. But there was one thought he couldn't put a halter on — a new echo: "Why? Why has the Lord come to me?"

"The prophetic signs are all there," said the cockroach. "But as always no one wants to see them. But, Joseph, look again: 'The sign of the Son of Man will appear in the sky! The elements will vanish with a roar, the earth melting away in a blaze, destroyed by fire.' Forty years ago the signs began to appear in the sky: over the desert of New Mexico, over Hiroshima, Bikini and Siberia! That's why I am here, Joseph. I have come to save you from death! Learn from me for I am everlasting. I am, as the ancients loved to call me, 'The Lord of Reck.' Not W-R-E-C-K but R-E-C-K. Blessed are those who hear my voice and enter my kingdom." The great black cockroach then took Joe by the hand and led him behind the refrigerator. As he followed, Joe's body miraculously began to shrink to fit the narrow, damp space. "The end, Joseph, is at hand. If you remain outside my kingdom, you will surely die. A human can absorb no more than a few hundred roentgens of radiation, but we cockroaches, the ones of the kingdom of life, can absorb over 60,000 such units of nuclear radiation. We will survive the holocaust — we are the sacred survivors. While the dinosaurs perished, we survive. We have survived war, plague, revolution, the Inquisition, DDT and even the Orkin Man. We are not only prehistoric, we *are* the future. Come, join us. Why be reckless and lose your life?"

"Of course," said Joe, "the Lord of Reck! That's an Old English word for 'caution,' the word once used for 'take care.' Today we hear only its opposite: 'reckless.' But I thought that you, Jesus, called us to put away the virtue of reck and to become reckless — to risk life in order to find it?"

"Joseph, Joseph, my son," came the forceful voice from the darkness behind the refrigerator. "Don't be stupid. I, your Lord, came to you tonight because you are different from the others out there. Each of them seeks to be a hero or heroine. That need is the primal push. The greatest problem in life is to earn self-esteem. It is the burning passion that blinds men and women — that thirst for glory. The paths of glory are mapped out by society, and the foolish masses follow like sheep, earning their tinseled trophies within the system. They are fools to give away their lives trying to be heroes," snickered the great cockroach in a husky voice.

"Yes, I am afraid that's the truth," said Joe. "But you, Jesus, called us to the greatest act of heroism: to give our lives for our friends, for those we love."

"Joseph, awaken from those illusions. Listen to the young people of your day — they know the truth! Why become a sacrifice in some president's private war? Why surrender to the madness of the sacrifices that society requires? Why give your life for a three-bedroom house in the suburbs, for a membership in a country club? Can't you see that all your noble ideas of heroism finally come to nothing but this?" The constant purr of the refrigerator motor hummed behind the hypnotic voice of the Lord of Reck as he spoke in a voice steeped with the conviction of thousands and thousands of years of survival as a non-hero.

Suddenly Joe cried out, "You are not the Christ — you are the Anti-christ! Your kingdom is safe all right, but it is also cramped, narrow and too small and dark for me. It is infested with the disease of security that castrates the human spirit. And Jesus said . . ."

"Don't quote Jesus to me," shouted back the cockroach, "as if you were some holier-than-thou preacherman! Show me a hero today in religion. The young know that today's Church is a barren womb for heroism. She supports the very system that makes her powerless. She is no mother of heroes. She's afraid to set herself against her own culture. The kingdom she preaches is no different than ours . . . ." Like thunder, peals of laughter rebounded in the dark canyon behind the refrigerator. As the laughter melted away in that pre-dawn hour, the voice of the great cockroach became soft, enticing and motherly: "Come, Joseph, follow me, and you will live forever!"

"Never! I choose to follow the Lord of Recklessness. I seek his kingdom and not yours. For your kingdom is composed of ex-heroes, drop-outs from the work of justice and peace, burned-out saints, ex-seekers on the quest for the Holy Grail, those who have mortgaged their dreams of greatness, ex-lovers afraid to love again. Those are the ones who follow you and hide in the wood-work of the kingdom of the Lord of Reck." As he spoke, Joe felt himself slowly returning to his normal size. With one mighty push he moved the refrigerator out into the center of the kitchen and stepped out of the darkness.

Visible through the kitchen window, the sun was now rising amidst clouds of scarlet and flaming orange. As the clouds, shot through with the brilliant rays of the rising sun, tumbled over one another, Joe mused, "It looks like an atomic bomb blast, but it's only sunrise." Standing there at his kitchen window as the yellow light of a new day flooded the floor, his reflections continued, "It's a new day and I am new. I'm going to live this day in an entirely new way." Joe brewed himself a cup of coffee and sat down quietly. As he drank it, looking out his kitchen window, he recalled words of St. Augustine that he had read long ago: "God creates the universe new every morning." "New!" said Joe aloud. Yes, creation was new and fresh. He, Joe Moss, was new; the world was new. And anything, yes, anything was possible.

When I opened my eyes, the dragon was gone, and it was sunset. The whole day had slipped away. The air in the old shed smelled like fireworks, like the breeze on the night of the Fourth of July.

I have written down these stories as well as I can remember them. And I close this log entry with a question: I'm like Joe Moss. Why me, Lord? Why is this all happening to me?

Saturday, March 29th

The day is cloudy and wet. The low grey sky helps me to be still. I've been waiting all week for Saturday and hoping for a chance to be alone again. Naturally, I hope that the dragon will come again, since I have some questions for him about the Lord of Reck. During the week I have wondered about how I hide from being hurt. I have begun to see how easy it is to let trivial concerns be an escape from reality: the many vain pursuits that, as the cockroach in the dragon's story said, occupy the human heroic spirit. The trivial is a painkiller that lets me ignore the shadow of nuclear destruction that hangs like a cloud over my home and the world. But unlike the cockroach's answer which seeks safety and only makes the human spirit smaller, heroism needs to expand to its true purpose. I have tried all week not to run away from the pain of sacrifices, choices and decisions but to embrace them instead. As I sit here writing, I must admit that I feel good about what has happened. I feel a slight change in my way of relating to Martha and the kids. They don't understand why I come here on Saturdays, but as long as I'm at home they don't seem to mind. Still, I think Martha is afraid that I'm having a nervous breakdown.

Today, before lunch, the dragon came again. Overjoyed, I threw open the door the minute I saw him looking through the small glass window. We shared some bread and a single apple. I was amazed that dragons don't eat as much as one might think.

We talked for some time about the Lord of Reck, heroism and the Quest, and at the end the dragon spoke. "The question still uppermost in your mind, George," he said, wiping the crumbs from his lips, is, 'Why the Quest? Why the Journey?' "

32

"Yes," I replied, "that's what keeps bobbing up and down in the dark pool of my mind like the Loch Ness Monster."

"The best answer to why one is sent," he continued, "can be found in a story. This is a tale from the very *beginning. It's actually from the Oldest Bible Never Written, and it's a story about how the earth came to be." Then he told me to close my eyes and let my imagination free as he began.*

In the beginning, when God first thought of creating the heavens and the earth, all was darkness. Actually when it came to mind, God was creating a great pot of cosmic soup. Slowly, as God stirred the fertile soup and toyed with the wonderful idea, a batch of procreative supernova chain reactions began to bubble and boil — and suddenly there was light! God was delighted with the result and called the light day, and the darkness that surrounded the light was named night. Thus evening came and with it the end of the very first day. But while night came, God did not rest. No, indeed! She was so elated that she sat up all night, wondering what she would create out of her great cosmic soup on the next day!

By dawn the soup was taking on a color and texture never seen before. With careful strokes God stirred, thickened and seasoned — and by noon God lifted the sky out of her formless but fertile soup. It took her all day to shape it, smoothing out the wrinkles until it was a beautiful blue dome. Thus came the evening of the second day. Elated with what had taken shape, God decided to go to her drawing board. She labored all that night with designs for what she would create next.

On the third day, God artistically created the earth, and upon it she poured all the oceans and seas. From her blueprints of the previous night, she shaped all kinds of vegetation: trees and seed-bearing plants, flowers, prairie grasses and crab-grass. And God looked upon all that she had created and saw that it was good — even the crab-grass! Evening came and the end of the third day, but God did not stop. She labored long over the decisions of what she would create tomorrow, experimenting with small working models of her ideas.

By morning on the fourth day, God was ready. All her experiments the night before had worked perfectly. And so she created quasars and giant nuclear reactors that she called "suns." She created billions of suns and sprinkled them throughout space; in playful exuberance she flung entire galaxies in all directions. But she saved one of the more beautiful suns and one lovely moon for the earth. And God looked upon what she had made and saw that it also was good. Evening came, and although God was tired, having hardly rested at all for three nights and four days, the beauty of the sun and the moon energized her. So she resisted the temptation to take a nap and returned to her drawing board.

All night, with a rush of excitement, God drew designs. This time her ideas required continuous modifications. The floor was littered with unused designs crumbled and rolled up into balls like paper moons; parts of experimental models lay here and there. As on all the previous nights, God had to restrain her desire to create what was really upmost in her heart, what all this previous work was only a preparation for.

Morning came on the fifth day, and with joy God saw that the first sunrise looked just as she had pictured it — a real work of art. But even before the sun rose, God was already busy creating fish, reptiles and dinosaurs — creatures of all sizes. God was delighted with her cockroach, making it almost indestructible. With pleasure, she listened to the chorus of birds singing. Her long hours of the night before had made possible this early morning concert. Keep in mind that it had been no easy task to create a different bird song for each of the over 9,000 different species of birds. Even Mozart (Wolfgang Amadeus, that is) would have found that commission impossible.

Evening came and God was tired but proud as Punch, for she could see that it was all good. That night God labored hunchbacked over her drawing board, humming a song under her breath — a special kind of song. Everything was ready, and she was eager to create the dream that had begun this entire process — the dream, the germ of an idea which she had lovingly placed into her great pot of cosmic soup.

When sunrise came on the sixth day, God greeted it feeling a bit sick. You see, she was pregnant — and early morning is a difficult time for expectant mothers! The delivery, shortly after sunrise, shook all creation with cosmic joy. God rocked her child in her arms, humming the song of the night before, the first lullaby. Growing in beauty and in size, the child was a toddler by midmorning. At noon God and her teenager had lunch together. And by early afternoon the earth-child was fully mature — tall, strong and fair.

God rejoiced in her fully grown child, but she could see that, although her child was happy, something was missing. Her child's cup was only half full! Something was wanting. Because she loved her child, God tried everything. She gave presents. She engaged in philosophical discussions and talked about music. God baked an apple pie. But still the cup of her child remained less than full; something was not right.

Now, it is always hard for a mother to see, no matter how much she loves her child, that love is not enough. God had never been happier than she was now on this sixth day — never in all the eons and eons of time — yet her child was still wanting. So in the middle of the afternoon of the sixth day, God returned to her drawing board. She began to work on a project that she really did not want to do but knew that she must. As the sun traveled into the last quarter of the western sky, and the long dark-fingered shadows announced that evening was approaching, God came outside looking for her child. She had a present that she knew would bring delight. Her child was absent-mindedly skipping flat stones across a pond and looked up idly as God approached.

"Close your eyes," God said. "Don't look — I've a present for you, dear." God told the child not to look because she knew that surprise is half of pleasure. But also God did not want her child to see the tears in her own eyes.

"Open your eyes now," God said. "Look what I have for you." And her child — flesh of her body, her heart's desire and greatest love — looked up and saw another person standing beside God, who was so lovely, so much the same — and yet not the same. "O mother," exclaimed her first child. "What a wonderful gift — my heart is so full it's overflowing!" "O mom, I'm so happy!" laughed the second child.

"Yes, I knew you would be," said God. And she was more proud of being able to bring happiness to her children than she had been when she designed her nuclear reactor suns. "But go now, children, and enjoy one another. Today is your birthday, and my gift to both of you is each other."

And so, hand in hand and madly in love, the

two walked off together, leaving God's garden. The sun, as red as the heart of a volcano, was slipping down behind the tree tops of paradise as God slowly, very slowly, began to walk away. She started toward the deepest part of the great forest at the center of paradise. God was tired — yes, ready to rest — but a sword of pain pierced her great loving heart. Her children, her beloved children, were now gone! Gone also was the intense pleasure she had known of her infant falling asleep in her arms, of holding her young child in her lap, of watching the poetry of the fully mature bodies of both children as they moved with such grace. But although God's heart felt the stab of the sword of separation, it also sang. The melody was a combination of every one of the bird songs and creature sounds she had composed on the fourth night. Her heart sang because she had really given her children two gifts: not simply someone to love but the freedom to love another! "What else," thought God, "what else can a mother do if she's really a mother?"

And so the sixth day ended as God walked deeper and deeper into the dense forest. The moon rose, full and yellow, over a distant jagged mountain range. God was so tired. "Yes," she thought, "tonight I will sleep, and all day tomorrow I will rest." She would be alone now. It was not easy, but she truly loved both of them, her most special creations, her children. And she knew that love requires giving away what you love. Yes, she would live alone now, until someday . . . someday her children would come home, would come back to her.

The parable tale was finished and silence flooded the garage. I sat with my eyes tightly closed, for they filled with tears when I thought of my children and how someday soon they would fall in love with someone and leave. Slowly I opened my eyes, and to my surprise the dragon was still in the room. The sun had set, and dark shadows crowded into the back room of the garage. Sitting in the shadows, hidden in the twilight darkness, sat my dragon friend.

"That's a beautiful story," I managed to say as a lone tear wandered down my cheek. "I want some time to think about it."

"Yes," said the dragon quietly, "that would be important. For it is love that calls you on this journey. It is love that makes the Quest a homecoming, and it is love that is your source of energy to continue on the Quest."

We both sat in silence a long time. Finally, the dragon said, "I think it's about time for supper; your wife will be wondering about you. It's time to return to the other track of your pilgrimage. Remembering how happy the earth-children were when they discovered each other, why don't you take Martha dancing tonight? Surprise her, Sent George, with a resurrection of romance.

"And here are a couple of gifts for you. They are mystical equipment for the Quest. Take them; you will need them," he said as he handed me an antique mirror in a battered silver frame, and a bag of books. With a gracious, knightly bow the dragon departed. And I will follow, closing the door of the shed on both the story and the gifts the dragon gave me.

Saturday, April 5th

Another rainy day, and I am alone in the garage. My wife finds these times of solitude impossible to understand, but she seems pleased about our new way of being together. I think she feels it's only a passing fad, and — who knows? — perhaps it is. Today, I examined the gifts the dragon left for me. The mirror is most unusual. Though it seems to be a mirror, nothing is visible when I look into it. Maybe it is magical, and I simply don't know how it works. The bag of books is most interesting. It contains the Bible and many other holy books: the Tao Te Ching *and the writings of* Confucius *and* Chuang Tzu *of China, the* Upanishads *and* Bhagavad Gita *of India, Buddha's* Dhammapada, *the* Koran *of Islam as well as writings of the North American Hopi Indians. I flipped through them, reading here and there, but I don't know why the dragon gave them to me. Most of them are beyond me, and I just don't understand them. My mind is as empty as that mysterious mirror. As the day passes, I eagerly wait for the dragon to explain it all.*

3:00 p.m.

No sign of the dragon yet. The day drags on slowly and I'm bored. I wonder if the dragon has a name, but these and other idle questions remain unanswered. I think I'll take a nap.

6:00 p.m.

Time for supper. For some reason he didn't come this Saturday. I'm confused. I feel like the day has been a failure. Maybe I did something wrong and wasn't

*in the right frame of mind. I looked in the mirror
he gave me just as I started to leave, and for the first
time I saw something — a vague sort of shadow for
a brief moment, then it disappeared. Strange.*

"TAKE THE GREAT BOW OF THE
SACRED WRITINGS AND PLACE
IN IT AN ARROW SHARP
WITH DEVOTION.
DRAW THE BOW
WITH CONCENTRATION...
AND HIT THE CENTER
OF THE MARK."

Mundaka Upanishads

Saturday, April 12th

I overslept this morning and didn't arrive at the garage until around ten. To my surprise — and delight — the dragon was waiting for me! I told him how disappointed I was that he didn't visit last Saturday. He only smiled and said, "To be alone is a good thing." Then he opened one of the books he had left, the gospel of Luke, and read to me from chapter 5. It was the story about Jesus going to the desert to be alone and to pray. "To be alone for certain times," the dragon said, "is to learn to see inside. Doing nothing forces you to taste your lack of power and self-sufficiency. That mirror, Sent George, is a hermitage mirror. Look into it and be alone; be quiet and you will see the shadow side of yourself which is usually invisible. You will see that what you consciously deny is there: the petty weaknesses, the fears and doubts, the desires, the flirtations with evil. This time by yourself can help you confront those things inside you which prevent your finding the Holy Grail. It takes great humility to look in that mirror and acknowledge that the face marred with those weaknesses is yours. The mirror is important, and so are these maps."

"What maps?" I asked, having searched the bag and found only holy books.

"These books are no ordinary books. They are not just containers of information and entertainment. No, Sent George, they are maps which will lead you to the Holy Grail." He reached into the bag and removed one of them, saying, "Why read commentaries written on commentaries, maps re-drawn from the original? Find the mystery in the original! Read between the lines, and you will be surprised at what you will find. But perhaps a story will help explain.

Close your eyes, George, and we'll go together on another adventure."

"Before we begin," I interrupted timidly, "could I ask a question?"

"A question?" asked the dragon. "What might that be, George?"

"I'm curious — do you, ah, er . . . do you have a name? It seems so impersonal to speak to you only as 'the dragon.' "

He smiled and replied, "Everything has a name, George, even the Divine Mystery. In fact, God is a millionaire when it comes to names. Nothing else in the world has so many names and yet remains so nameless. Among the ancients, to know a person's name was to hold power over him or her, and so people like the pharaohs of Egypt had two names: one by which they were commonly known and another secret name, known only to their most intimate friends. Then the gods of death would have no power over them. So do you want my real name or the name by which I am commonly known?"

I paused, aware that this was no insignificant question. After some thought I replied, "Tell me the name you would like me to call you."

The dragon flashed an expansive smile and said, "I am known as the Celestial Dragon of the Jade Throne, the Imperial Treasurer of the Chest of Wisdom, the Benevolent Guardian of Pilgrims, Seekers and Lost Children. I have ten thousand names — but you, George, may call me Igor Dragomirov, or just Igor if you wish."

I was stunned. "You're Russian?" I asked in disbelief. Indeed, I thought, he is a red dragon, but I never . . . I mean a Communist as a friend! "Igor," I said, hoping to hide my shock, "you're a pre-revolutionary dragon — I mean you're very old, so you must be beyond politics and. . . "

Igor interrupted my stammering. "Does it make

*any difference, George, whether I am a Democrat or
a Communist, a Taoist or a relic of the Ming Dynasty,
as long as we are friends? Aren't those on the Quest
citizens of a greater world, members of a family
which includes all nations, ideologies and creeds?
George, you and I are becoming friends. It's a long
process to become a true friend to someone. Let's
leave all that propaganda and discrimination behind
— it's just so much unnecessary baggage in life. Can't
we just be friends?"*

*I was ashamed of my small heart and the nar-
row limits of my mind. "Yes, Igor, let's be friends.
Knowing your name will make it much easier to be
your friend. Igor . . . Igor . . . I like the sound of it.
It's a good name for a red dragon," I said with a
laugh. "Now tell me the story you promised." I closed
my eyes and leaned back in my chair.*

It was the Review Board weekend in heaven, and
God had once again convened his committee of
angels to review the activities of creation. God was
at the head of a long conference table, and a committee of angels and archangels was seated around
it. Each had a manila folder containing reports on
the various aspects of creation. These Review
Board meetings were times of great importance
and excitement, for it was at these meetings that
God presented new ideas for the evaluation of the
angelic committee.

"Before we go over our reports," God said with
a smile, "I would like to ask your opinions on an
idea that came to me the other night." Several
angels nodded their heads, while others moved
restlessly in their chairs. They were uneasy
whenever God began this way because it required
a diplomat's skill to discuss an idea that wasn't
practical. Naturally, some angels agreed with

every idea that God presented, even with the ones that were, to put it plainly, more than impractical, they were dumb — but, mind you, divinely dumb!

God wore a big smile, which only made the more conservative angels very nervous. They had learned over the millennia that the larger the smile, the more outlandish was the idea.

"I feel," said God, "that it's time for me to speak more directly to my children on earth. Until now I have spoken to them by means of a flood, fire, rainbows and, of course, a quiet whisper in the heart of certain chosen ones. But I feel that they need to hear more directly from me — to let them know the feelings of my heart, my dreams and my ideas on how to correct the problems they always seem to be getting themselves into. So . . . ," and here God paused and smiled again, "I think I should come to earth in human form, as one of them!"

Gasps and moans rose from around the conference table. The more timid angels quickly opened their manila folders and began nervously shuffling through their reports. God chuckled inwardly. He hadn't seen such a response from the Celestial Committee since he had sprung his idea of creating Adam on them.

One of the angels finally spoke. "Lord God, your idea certainly has merit. But don't we already have in place an excellent system for any messages you might want to send to earth? You have us, your angelic messengers who are willing to fly anywhere at any hour. Why do we need a *new* form of communication?"

"Too limited and too exclusive," responded God. "And it usually frightens the mortals when one of you angels suddenly materializes in front of them. No, we need a better means of reaching as many of them as possible."

"Lord God," suggested another angel on the committee, "your idea is intriguing. But I fear that it is not time yet for you to come to earth as one of them. My opinion, from all the reports I've seen, is that it will take at least three thousand more years before any such idea should be tried, and even then . . . " But the angel was interrupted by a chorus of voices.

"Lord God," chimed in an earnest archangel, "to come in human form would be beneath your dignity. And if you come, Lord, which race would you choose? Think of the complications of even the choice of skin color! Imagine how the others would feel if you single out one race: the resentment and envy, not to mention the charge of a 'special friendship.' "

"And, Lord God," spoke another voice, a deep bass voice that drowned out all the others, "which sex would you choose? Consider well such folly and how it will cause untold theological problems. Think of the discrimination; one sex will deeply resent the implication that you so favor the other."

At this point the committee members began to argue vigorously with one another, and one whispered, "Well, Yahweh's done it again — we might as well junk the agenda of this meeting!" ·

"Friends, friends . . . quiet, please, quiet!" said God. "I hear your many objections and concerns. Indeed the problems you raise are valid. It's just that I'm so impatient, so eager to see my creation become what I dream it can. Perhaps I *am* in too great a hurry to resolve the first-stage problems of my wonderful experiment of Adam and Eve. You are probably correct in thinking it may take another three or four thousand years before they will be ready. And if I hear you correctly, some of you feel that the problems of *which* sex, race or nationality to choose may make it an eternal impossible dream."

The silence that followed was like that of many a meeting — a blend of disappointment and frustration for some, a sense of victory for others and questions still hanging in the air. The static stillness around the conference table was broken by the voice of one angel. "My Lord God, why not come to earth in the form of writing? Your children, the Sumerians, have perfected the earlier experiments of expressing messages and ideas by making marks, by the use of symbolic figures. And the Egyptians and Chinese are making some rather remarkable breakthroughs in its technology. You could come to earth in the form of hieroglyphics — as letters of the alphabet!"

"Marvelous idea," shouted God, "marvelous . . . yes, that's it! I will come as letters of the alphabet. I shall come as word!"

"But Lord God," said the bass-voiced angel, "which alphabet will you be? Egyptian, Chinese, Hittite, Hebrew or Greek? Isn't that the same problem as having to choose between the races? No, Lord God, you cannot be partial! You cannot discriminate and still be God! At least not if you are to be who you are — the God of all of them! No, you must stay with the old ways and continue to speak to them in flood, fire and the rainbow. These are universal containers for your messages. We have no need for any novel forms. The old will continue to serve us well." As the angel finished, a short burst of applause expressed the agreement of many.

Under the conference table, unseen by the members of the Review Board, God's foot tapped in anger and impatience. If the angels had seen the divine toe tap-tap-tapping, they easily would have decoded it's message: "Why are they so afraid of anything new and untried? They think

47

that Adam was a big mistake; but I think a bigger one was the creation of committees!"

In the silence that followed, all faces were turned toward the head of the table where God sat with closed eyes, lost in deep thought. Slowly God opened one eye, then the other — and looked directly at the angel who had proposed that God come to earth as letters in the alphabet and who, at this point, was nervously chewing at the end of a yellow pencil. "You say that this invention of writing has great potential?" asked God. "Can we rightly foresee that they will continue to improve on their earlier experiments and that some day everyone will be able to read? And that by means of written words they will be able to understand the most abstract of ideas?"

"Yes, Lord God," replied the angel. "With written words you could prepare them for your coming in human form. You could speak without causing the fear of your thunderbolt messages and more clearly than using rainbows, which can mean almost anything. But my distinguished angelic colleague, I fear, is correct. You would have to choose one of many alphabets. No, I withdraw my suggestion; it is of no value."

"Far from it, my clever friend," responded God, who once again was wearing a wide, expansive grin. "Far from it! Because I have decided — after careful consideration of your suggestions and objections — I have decided to come into the world as ink!"

"INK?" gasped the angels.

"Yes, Ink!" replied God. "Then I can reside in the letters of *all* alphabets. I shall come to earth in the alphabets of the Egyptians and the Hebrews, in Chinese and Sanskrit, in Greek and Latin, in Russian and . . . well, the possibilities are unlimited . . . unlimited!"

And here our parable ends, except for this brief postscript. God did indeed come into the world as ink. And the people of earth recognized the Divine Presence in the Hebrew letters of the *Torah*, in the Sanskrit of the Vedic books of India and in the Chinese characters of the *Tao Te Ching*. With reverence they bowed before the Arabic letters of the *Koran* and illuminated the Greek and Latin of the Gospels with gold leaf. Just as God said at that Review Board meeting, "The possibilities are unlimited."

When he had finished, Igor's long claw tapped the top book on the pile and he said, "Learn to be quiet in your heart, and you will learn to hear the messages in these books. You will hear more than words, more than philosophical truth; if you learn to be quiet, you will hear the Author, George. You will hear the Ink, and it will guide you on your quest. Trust in that truth. Trust."

"THE HEARING OF THE SPIRIT
IS NOT LIMITED TO ANY
ONE FACULTY, TO THE EAR
OR TO THE MIND;
IT DEMANDS THE EMPTINESS
OF ALL THE FACULTIES...

THEN
THE
WHOLE
BEING
LISTENS."

The Way of
Chang Tzu

Saturday, April 19th

Here I am in my hermitage, trusting that the Author will speak to me. Reflecting on the dragon's parable about God as ink has radically changed the way I think about people of other religions. I find it increasingly difficult to use the words "pagan" or "heathen"; they have lost their meaning. Now I have begun to see how universal the search is. I feel a comradeship with people in other parts of the world who are searching too. Today, as I look in my hermitage mirror, I see something ugly I have never seen before. It's an image of myself as superior to others, more loved by God, more important. It's a disturbing view of a side of me that I haven't been aware of. With each hour alone I am beginning to see more of my hidden self. The most surprising part is that I'm learning to love even that dark side of myself.

Martha wanted to spend this weekend visiting her family, but I said that it was impossible, that I had to spend Saturday here. I feel that such discipline is essential for my quest. Some things you can be flexible about, but some don't allow any latitude. When my friend Igor arrived, he knew somehow what had happened between Martha and me, and this is the tale he told.

After God had created the earth and the heavens, all the animals and birds and Adam and Eve, God retired from the hard work of creation. During the week after creation, God went to visit Adam and Eve, who lived in a little grass shack under the great apple tree.

"Well, children," God said, "how are things going? Is everything O.K.?"

"Oh yes, indeed," replied Adam. "Everything is fine. Eve and I love all that you have made."

"Yes," added Eve, "it *is* good; however . . . ," and Adam shot a quick, fearful glance her way as she continued, "it's kind of stuffy here in the garden. The air's so still."

"Hmmm. . . ," replied God, looking around, "I hadn't noticed. Well, dear, nothing is perfect in *this* life. But I'm retired, you know. Next time I create a world, I will have to work out that little problem. See you later, children. Enjoy yourselves!"

Two days later, God came to visit again. Adam and Eve were sitting on the front steps of their little grass shack. God greeted them as usual: "Well, children, how are things going?"

"Just fine, God," replied Eve as she held Adam's hand.

God looked at Adam, "And you, my son?"

"Oh, it's O.K., God, but there's nothing to do in the evening after we've worked in the garden all day."

"Hmmm . . . ," said God, "I never thought about that as a problem — I mean, having *nothing* to do. I'm rather enjoying it in my retirement these days. But let's see — perhaps you could dance!"

"Dance?" said both Adam and Eve together. "Maybe the birds and the bees dance as a mating act, but it's so *animal*! Oh no, Lord, it isn't proper for us *humans* to dance."

"Well . . . ," said God, "it was just an idea. I'm only trying to find something that would not force me to come out of retirement and yet would make the two of you happy. If you were happy, perhaps I would feel better about creation." God looked down at the ground, and a large divine toe played in the dust.

Adam asked, "What's wrong, God? I can see

52

that you've got something on your mind. What is it?"

"Well," said God, "you see, I have been visited by a delegation of dinosaurs. They are upset because the two of you are living together but aren't married. *They* say that it's a scandal and the talk of the whole garden. I told them that they weren't married either, but they only replied — all in chorus, mind you — that they are only animals but that you two are humans!"

"Married?" asked Eve. "What's that?"

"It is, my dear," said God, "a ritual of becoming one for life."

"God, who needs marriage?" replied Adam. "Unless it's something that will make the garden less stuffy or is someplace to go for fun after the sun has gone down. And besides, God, why do you listen to those uptight dinosaurs? Their ideas are so old and outdated; they're so conservative and afraid to change. One of these days it will be the death of them!"

"Yes, Adam," said God, "I know. I've warned them about their conservative attitudes, but I have to listen to them. Both of you know how much weight they throw around in the garden. I have resisted coming out of retirement, but it looks like we're not going to have any peace in the garden until I create marriage." So God went to the drawing board and designed a beautiful ritual that two human beings could celebrate together.

On Saturday, Adam and Eve got married. It was a garden wedding, and all creation attended. The dinosaurs sat together in a group and twisted and turned their long necks to see who was present. They nodded continuously, approving of this "proper" ceremony for two people "living together." God also was present, smiling because finally everyone seemed to be happy and at peace.

Sunday morning, the second seventh day in history, God awoke with a shock. "I didn't give them a wedding present! What can I do? It's Sunday morning and everything is closed except the 7-11 store — and what kind of wedding gift can you get there?" With brush in hand God began to comb her hair, pondering the problem: "What on earth can I give them for a wedding present?"

About mid-morning all the creatures in the garden were startled to hear a giant crack of thunder that shot across the cloudless sky like a sonic boom. They all knew what it meant: God had just had an idea. The dinosaurs groaned and looked at each other with soulful eyes. "Oh dear, another new idea, another change!"

Since it was Sunday, Adam and Eve were sitting on their front steps doing nothing, as was the custom on the seventh day, when a great package wrapped in silver paper with a wonderful pink-ribboned bow slowly floated down out of the sky. The large, beautifully wrapped box came to earth directly in front of the two. Adam opened the card and read aloud, "Congratulations and best wishes to both of you. Love, Your God."

Quickly, they undid the wrappings and opened the box. Looking inside, the saw NOTHING! "What a strange wedding gift," they said to each other. "The box is empty!" But even as they spoke, the pink ribbon that was on the ground stood up and swayed to and fro in a delightful little dance. And the wrapping-paper stood up, whirled around and skipped off down the lawn. Something strange was going on. Something new was present in the garden, but whatever it was . . . it was invisible!

The leaves on their stems began to dance, swaying back and forth. The tall grasses with their long seed stems also began to move. Eve, her voice filled with excitement, cried out, "Look Adam, it's no longer so stuffy here in the garden. I feel a gentle touch on my skin that's cool and delightful." At that moment, a white, puffy parachute-like seed head floated by as if it were adrift on an invisible river. Heavy with sperm, it nodded to the honeymooners, who stood in astonishment in front of their grass shack.

Then, invisible fingers played in the hair of the young couple, causing their locks to gently fall about their shoulders and flow outward. Adam looked at Eve, and Eve looked at Adam . . . "Let's dance — like the ribbon, like the leaves and the grasses — let's dance!"

And so it was that on the second seventh day God created the wind. It was a most special creature, for it was a vital part of God herself. She had let her hair down, and in an act of great sensuality was slowly stroking the body of her creation with her hair! That act of love set seeds airborne, gave coolness to the garden, carried scents and perfumes aloft, caused lifeless flags to flutter. The gift flapped Buddhist prayer-flags in the cold, blue air of Tibet and sent sailing ships dancing across the tops of the waves. And even to this day, so many millions of years afterward, each time we feel our hair being "let down by the wind," we too are called to freedom, to the dance and joy of life!

Igor finished his tale and sat gazing out the window. "Well, friend," I said, "you've done it again. I get the point: to be a pilgrim on the High Road I must learn to bend, to let my hair down — even to give up a precious Saturday in my hermitage if Love calls me to it. But I still don't think it will be easy to decide when to be flexible and when to remain true to my commitments!"

"True, Sent George," he replied. "But keep in mind that nowhere in all those books," and here his arm swept toward the pile of holy books on the table, "does it say that it will be easy. On the contrary, it is difficult and painful. It requires continuous balancing of needs and priorities. But once you have accepted the fact that it isn't going to be easy, you will be amazed at how much less difficult it becomes."

With those words he patted my shoulder with a great claw, said good-bye and left. I stayed in the garage for some time after that, allowing the story to soak into my heart. Now as I close up the room, I am ready to return to track two of my pilgrimage with a new heart . . . and a lighter spirit.

"A TREE THAT IS
UNBENDING
IS EASILY
BROKEN..."

Tao
Te
Ching

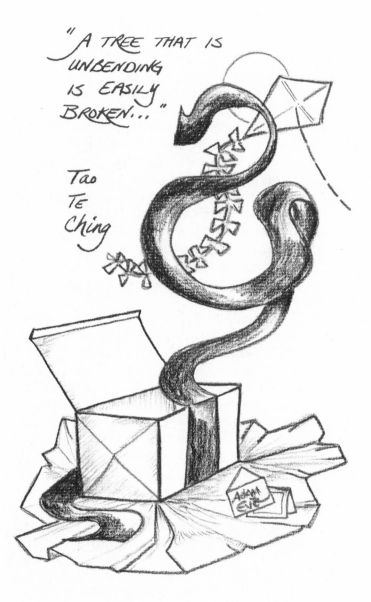

Saturday, April 26th

It's 1:30 and I just came in. I walked the razor's edge of priorities this morning and chose to respond to my son, who was involved in a project at school and needed me to help him with it. I trusted that I wouldn't miss seeing the guru-dragon if I didn't get here until after lunch. I suppose I could have spent the rest of the day doing something else, but I figured that half a day of solitude is better than none at all. Igor told me several weeks ago that Jesus went frequently to his own "garage," that special private place in the mountains outside his village. And Buddha had a tree he would sit under to be quiet and pray. But how did they pray? Did they "say prayers," or what? And didn't they have other people who needed them and wanted to spend time with them? Furthermore, I'm no Buddha or Jesus: I'm just plain George, regardless. . .

"Regardless of what, Sent George?" came a voice from behind me. There he was, big as life, smiling at me as he finished my thought out loud, "regardless of whatever that dragon might say!"

"I see that you're wondering how to balance your prayer time with the time you need for your wife and family," he said, reading my mind as usual. "Let me help you understand with a very short story about a heavenly poker game!

After the Lord God had created the world and all that was to live upon it and had divided time into seven days, the Devil came demanding his share of time. God proposed that they divide the week equally, each taking three and one-half days. But the Devil proposed instead that they play poker

58

for the possession of the days. Now God knew that the Devil always cheated when he played poker, but God just smiled and asked for a new deck of cards. The Devil insisted that the stakes for the first game be the first and last days of the work week. With his usual cheating, the Devil won the first game. Gathering up his winnings, he said to himself, "Ah, I can get each week off to a bad start by putting folks on the wrong foot. I can instill competition and other vices on the first day of the week, and with the last day I can show them delicious ways to 'let their hair down' after a weary week of labor." Game followed game, and God allowed the Devil to win six whole days! Only one day remained — and God, with a riverboat gambler's flourish, laid out a royal flush on the table and won the seventh day.

As the Devil walked away from the green-topped card table, he chuckled to himself, "Great winning odds, six to one! With such odds I can't help but win the world."

As God rose from the table, a circle of angels who had watched the card game shook their heads in dismay. "Why, Lord God," they said, "did you let that cheating Devil win six of the seven days? What can you do with only one day?"

And God answered, "Oh, I've got special plans. I need only one day; that's more than enough!"

An angel exclaimed, "Of course, we should have guessed. One day full of prayer and worship will give your children the strength they need to remain faithful to you for the other six."

God smiled. "That wasn't exactly what I had in mind," he said. "All I need is one day for them to *enjoy* me! They can savor *me* when they enjoy leisure, when they rest. For it is only then that they can recognize and return the love that I have put into all creation — which is stronger than all the

Devil's daily temptations. Once they learn how to love through rest and play, the Devil won't have a chance!"

As the story ended, I laughed and said, "Martha and the kids would certainly agree with that story! You should see how much easier it is to love each other since we've learned how to rest and play. And my quiet times are at the bottom of it all."

"Yes," said Igor, "you are finding the secret to keeping the Sabbath holy, whether it's Saturday or Sunday or — in the case of our Moslem friends — Friday!"

"I think I understand all that pretty well," I said, "but there's another question that's bothering me. I've been reading in the Bible that God hears the prayers of the just. How do I know whether I am just? And what good does it do to pray if God doesn't hear my prayers?"

"Greater minds than yours have pondered the mystery of the saved and the damned," Igor replied. "Ah, yes, Sent George, does God listen only to the prayers of the 'just' and the 'pious'? I remember a story about a town and a flood — if you have time for another parable today."

"Since the last one was so short, fire away!" I said, and leaned back in my old rocker with my eyes closed.

Rock Springs, a sleepy Western town, awoke after fifty years of sober slumber to find that it had mushroomed overnight. The discovery of oil had been the magnet for hundreds and hundreds of house-trailers, campers and domesticated, old yellow school buses which now became the instant suburbs of Rock Springs. When the once-quiet town discovered oil, *it* was discovered by gamblers, prostitutes, drug pushers, bartenders and porno dealers. These entrepreneurs of sin and sex seemed to appear only moments after the arrival of multitudes of rough and tough oil field workers, fortune seekers and job hunters.

The brand-new bars and brothels of the now sleazy, neon-lit "Sodom City" made nighttime louder and livelier than day. But where there is sin, can salvation be far behind? Noah T. Brown, preacher and man of God, with a small gold cross on one lapel and an American flag on the other, opened a church of God at the far end of the neoned, sin-soaked Main Street. The large, square, sterile white frame building, with its stuck-on steeple, was a lighthouse in a sea of sin.

One evening, while midstream in a Bible Revival, as the organist and choir rendered the hymn "God is the Rock of My Salvation," Noah T. Brown heard a voice in his hairy inner ear. The message was one he had been expecting for some time: "ON JUNE 5, AT 5:13 P.M. GOD WILL DESTROY THIS CITY OF SIN!" While most would have shivered, Noah Brown was delighted! For him, messages of doom were a pure delight to deliver. And preach he did, his white beard electric with energy, his eyes aflame with saintly static. "REPENT, SINNERS, THE END IS NOW AT HAND!" he cried to Rock Spring's new citizens.

The divine forecast for June 5th, 5:13 p.m. did not dim the night-lights or high-life of Rock Springs; on the contrary, it fueled the fun. Gamblers offered great odds on the appearance of the Divine Destruction. Bars offered a new drink called "5:13" — an end-of-the-world combination of three shots of tequila and two of gin with a chaser of beer. And the other "house," the one at the opposite end of town, announced a two-for-one Happy Hour from 5 to 10 p.m. on June 5th. The other "house," located on a hill at the east end of Rock Springs, which was cradled in a valley ringed by mountains, was called Toad Hall — why, no one could remember. It was a two-and-one-half story, white Victorian mansion. Toad Hall was the best little whorehouse in the West, or so its satisfied customers claimed.

Five days before June 5th it began to rain. Everyone rejoiced, since it had been dry all spring. Ranchers and farmers came to town, joining oil workers and the rest who were unable to work because of the rain. The bars and pleasure domes operated at peak capacity both day and night. As the rainy days continued without a break, conversation began to center around the big dam located high up in the canyon. The rain had melted the snows on the peaks, and the run-off along with the pouring rain had swollen the streams. Where would it all go?

The Day of Doom, June 5th, arrived, wearing grey. As the clouds continued to dump endless rain on muddy, wet Rock Springs, the church was filled with the prayerful, good folks of the town, waiting for the fateful moment of 5:13. Its doors stood wide open in welcome, and Noah T. Brown, standing on the front steps, offered salvation to all who passed, but not one new person entered the church. At the other end of town Toad Hall, specially decorated and outlined with multicolored Christmas-tree lights, was filling up for the big party! Mrs. Thompson and her young ladies had also festooned its wide, circling porches with Japanese lanterns and gaudy red and yellow crepe paper streamers.

At 4:30 p.m. the town siren blew, announcing that it had become necessary to open the flood gates of the dam. This added influx of water caused the already bank-full streams to overflow, sloshing into Main Street. Within minutes it was ankle deep. At 5:08 p.m., above the sound of rock music blasting from the bars and brothels, and the even louder organ, tambourine and guitar music from the church, arose the sound of a great cracking and crumbling. As the sound grew to a thunderous roar, everyone knew what it was. The giant concrete dam, high in the canyon, was breaking apart!

Noah T. Brown stepped inside his church, closed the doors and barred them as gamblers with drinks in hand, drug dealers with pockets full of coke and grass, liquored oil workers, adulterous ranchers with half-naked hookers on their arms, and just plain fun-loving sinners raced for the church. They pounded their fists on its doors, but Noah was deaf to their cries. Over the roar of the tidal wave now crashing down the narrow canyon, he shouted, "You all had your chance to repent; now reap the harvest of your sins!"

Finding the entrance barred, the crowd of sinners turned toward the other end of Main Street as someone shouted, "Toad Hall on the hill!" Mrs. Thompson helped them as they ran, stumbling and scrambling, up the front steps into her already-crowded house. Behind them a towering tidal wave burst forth from the mouth of the canyon into Rock Springs, with log cabins, rocks and tall fir trees tumbling end over end in its crest.

The sinful night-people of Rock Springs held each other fearfully and cried out in the face of the roaring waters, "Lord, have mercy on us!"

Across town the first waves of water were smashing against the church, as old Noah led his people in prayers of gratitude. "DO NOT SWEEP ME AWAY WITH SINNERS, IN WHOSE HANDS

ARE EVIL PLOTS . . .AS FOR ME, I WALK THE PATH OF PERFECTION . . . PSALM 25." Their faces, starched stiff with sanctity, lit up as tongues of fire descended upon them. Filled with zeal, they cried out, "GOD WAS RIGHT, WE WERE RIGHT — WE ARE RIGHT!" Aflame with holy frenzy, Noah T. Brown whipped open the closet door, revealing a tall, black iron lever, as he shouted, "My mommy didn't have any dumb kids!" With a great WHAM, Noah's church sprang loose from its foundation, while beneath the church, giant pontoons instantly inflated with air.

The destruction, total and absolute, of the city of Rock Springs, took less than five minutes and was completed by 5:18 p.m. on June 5. Nothing remained of the city or its people; gone were the oil rigs, trailer houses, bars, stores and homes. A great, silent, muddy lake now filled the valley from mountainside to mountainside. And floating on the vast brown lake was a single house.

Those inside, white and breathless with shock, stood in awed, solemn silence as they looked upon the still, muddy lake. And all that could be heard above the lapping of the waters was the sound of the wind as it flapped the tattered and torn Japanese paper lanterns that hung from the porch of Toad Hall.

"HAS THE NEWS OF THE OVERWHELMING
DAY OF JUDGEMENT REACHED
YOU? WHEREFORE WARN YOUR
PEOPLE..."

Mohammed
The Koran

"REFORM YOUR LIVES!
THE KINGDOM OF HEAVEN
IS RIGHT AT HAND."

Jesus
The Gospel of
Matthew

When I opened my eyes it was dark. Igor was gone, and only the aroma of fireworks' smoke remained in my tiny room. I put things away and got ready to go to the house. As I started to leave, I felt an unusual sense of power surging through me. I found myself whispering, "Help me, Lord, I am a sinner, and I don't think I'm able to pull it off by myself. Help me to be a good husband and a good father." There are spring flowers blooming in the yard around my garage — beautiful and promising.

Saturday, May 3rd

Spring is everywhere. The birds are returning, and there's the excitement in the air of life exploding in every direction. I am seeing spring this year as never before. I think it's because I can feel spring within myself. My wife, my family and the people at work have all said that I'm different: more patient, more relaxed, more peaceful. If they only knew that inside of me the conflicts seem heightened, as if some great power were struggling to get out, to explode. If the dragon and all these books are right and there is a God-seed inside each of us, then what would happen if this seed could be cracked open and all that energy released?

Late in the morning Igor dropped by. I always wonder if the neighbors or my wife see him as he flies in. Or does he come walking up the driveway? I only see him when he's standing at the door. Who knows, maybe I'm the only one who sees him. He told me another story about "the beginning." I didn't realize there could be so many, but he assured me there have been countless beginnings, and each has its own story. Today he told me the tale of God splitting the Adam.

God had taken the day off and was lounging in a large, green canvas lawn chair in the center of creation. Clustered around God were several arch-angels, and together they were admiring what had been accomplished in only six short days. Paradise was alive with activity as birds of all colors and shapes flew from tree to tree, filling the air with a multitude of marvelous melodies. Creatures of all sizes and descriptions moved gracefully among

67

the clusters of wildflowers heavy with blossoms.

God sipped a tall, frosted glass of lemonade, looked out over all that had been created and said, "Hmmm, that's good . . . but, it could be better!" Like any truly great artist, God was not satisfied with the finished work of art and wanted to make some changes. As the old saying goes, "It takes two to create a masterpiece: the artist to create the work of art, and someone to shoot him when it's finished; otherwise, he'll keep changing it until it's ruined." Even God was not immune to this habit and was "itching" to make some changes in creation.

The cluster of archangels looked nervously at one another as God said, "I think I should change just a few things here and there; it just doesn't look right. Something's missing."

"Gee, Lord," spoke up the Archangel Michael, "it sure looks fine to me. You've got variety, color, excellent design — and it all fits together perfectly. It's so well organized and so peaceful."

"You've hit upon it, Michael," said God, alive with excitement. "That's the problem: it's just too orderly. There's no spontaneity! You don't get any sense of energy. What's missing is the dynamic element. Take Adam, for example. Look at him over there. See what I mean?"

"What's wrong?" asked Michael. "He's a masterpiece. Look at the perfection of line and form in his body, his ability to think and create. The hands, too — marvelous idea, marvelous! He is so complete and self-contained. He's a solar system unto himself."

"That's right, Michael," responded God. "Artistically he's perfect, and he's in full harmony with all the rest of creation. But he's not dynamic; he lacks inner energy. But what to do? I will have to sleep on the problem."

The very next day God appeared at the weekly staff meeting, and with delight dancing on every word, announced, "I have solved the problem. Naturally, at this point my solution is only a theory. But, relatively speaking, it's a good theory. And it is also theoretically possible even if I am a bit hesitant because of the potential danger involved."

"Danger?" echoed the angelic staff with one voice. For you see, in all the work of creating the cosmos up to this point, there had never been anything dangerous about it.

"Yes," said God, "my idea is still in the theory stage; no one has ever done it before. If my calculations are correct, it is possible that in the process of correcting my original design we might expect a rather, ah, um . . . ahem . . . enormous explosion. What I am proposing is . . . ," and here God paused, looking at each of the anxious angels seated around the conference table, "what I am proposing is to split my Adam!"

A gasp of disbelief escaped from the shocked angels. Raphael said, "O my God, think of the consequences: radiation, nuclear winds, fire storms, mutations and untold cosmic disturbances!"

"Yes, Lord God," added Michael hastily, "dismiss the idea; it's just too dangerous. Look around you — everything is heavenly. Split the Adam and all hell will break loose!"

The Archangel Gabriel continued, "And remember, God, that at this point you only have one model with which to experiment. What if your theory is, ah . . . wrong? What if you split your Adam and destroy the only human being in existence in the process? Personally, I vote against it."

God arched a large eyebrow at the word "vote," and Gabriel hurriedly excused himself to go to the restroom. Looking at the others, God said, "Nope, my mind is made up. If you aren't ready to risk, you'll never taste life, and nothing creative or beautiful will ever happen. I'm taking the risk; tomorrow morning we will attempt to split the Adam."

The archangels shuffled out of the conference room, shaking their heads and speaking in hushed undertones. Some proposed a massive anti-nuclear demonstration that night outside God's big house, complete with candlelight procession, placards and folk singers. Others proposed that a delegation representing the various ranks of angels and all the creatures in the garden should attempt to convince God that the risk was too great, that the plan should be abandoned.

Now the only one in all creation who didn't know what was going on was Adam himself. God had strictly forbidden anyone to tell Adam of the Divine Theory of Relativity. And so Adam was busy naming the fish and animals and caring for the garden. That night he fell asleep as usual, like a child.

In the purple pre-dawn darkness, as Adam dreamed away in a deep sleep, the Lord God knelt over him with an upraised silver hammer. Like a master jeweler poised over a goose-egg sized diamond, the Lord God hovered over Adam, calculating at what precise angle and speed the blow should fall. And just before the sun rose, God split his Adam.

Adam's cry of separation seared the pre-dawn silence, and the roar was deafening. That cry of pain, created by the splitting of Adam, was to echo in every cry of pain thereafter — for all pain is born of separation or the fear of it. As a massive orange-red fireball ballooned skyward, God looked down on the split Adam and saw — half

70

an animal and half a human, half an adult and half a child, half a saint and half a sinner, half a man and half a woman. The one and only, the beloved Adam, was now not one but two. He was no longer complete, whole or self-contained, no longer a balanced solar system unto himself. In that historic split-second, Adam was instantly transformed from a gardener to an explorer — not in search of far-off romantic lands, but a seeker after his lost half-self. Adam was to be perpetually hungry for completion, friendship and for union.

As a giant, grey mushroom-shaped cloud filled the blue sky above the treetops of Paradise, nuclear winds of cyclone force blasted outward in all four directions as the atmosphere snapped and crackled with electric energy. The Archangel Michael, hanging on with both hands to the great Tree of Life in the center of the garden, shouted over the deafening roar, "And, Lord God, what shall we call this newest creation — this electrifying energy?"

"I think," God shouted back, white hair streaming in the wind, face beaming with the sweet smile of success, "I think I'll call it LOVE."

Late to dinner — no time to reflect on today's visit.

Saturday, May 10th

Last week's parable about love gave me a lot to think about. Love has many expressions, and the most beautiful are always gifts. But the more precious the gift, the more difficult it is to give it. As I thought about this, my friend and mentor arrived. With a swish of his great scaled tail Igor seated himself in the corner of the room and smiled. Dragons have great smiles, but they also have many more teeth to smile with! We chatted awhile about the coming of spring, the annual season for lovers and poets. Then we spent some time just sitting. We shared the prayer of the heart by simply sitting quietly together. After about twenty minutes he leaned back and blew a smoke ring upward. As it reached the ceiling it began to expand outward like a doughnut-shaped cloud. When it spread to the four corners, he said, "Today I have a story for you about another kind of love." And then he began . . . .

The sun rose that morning with a special splendor over the small provincial village of Nazareth. Joachim and Anne were eager to make it a day to remember, for it was the twelfth birthday of their only child, a daughter. For years they had saved money from their meager income to be able to purchase a birthday gift that would be equal to the occasion.

Joachim wandered with a lighthearted step down the narrow village street that led to the shops in the marketplace. Under his belt was the small bag of coins he would use to buy the birthday gift. Anne had given him enthusiastic instructions: "It must be a special and beautiful gift for our Mary!'' His heart was full of joy as he thought of his daughter. Was it just a father's pride, or was she truly a unique young woman? His little Mary was so uncomplicated, so full of beauty! Anne called her ''pure,'' but he wasn't sure what that meant. His Mary was indeed direct and childlike — yet she seemed so assured for her age.

As he entered the marketplace, Joachim saw that quite a crowd had gathered. A friend rushed up to him, saying, ''Joachim, come quickly, an Assyrian traveling merchant is in our market this morning. He's on his way to Jerusalem and then on to Egypt. Oh, what wonderful things he has to sell!'' Joachim smiled and said under his breath, ''Blest be the Lord our God who gives such gifts to us.''

In the center of the marketplace, surrounded by a crowd of villagers, stood a majestic Assyrian. His black beard was long, cut off square at the bottom and braided, bearing the scent of patchouli. Around him were bundles and boxes bursting with bright and enticing objects. ''Come closer, my friends,'' spoke the Assyrian, who was richly robed in red and gold. ''Before your very eyes are Greek fashions and vanities, tantric toys from far-off Tibet, cloth of gold from Persia, Syrian clothing woven from feathers of exotic birds, apocalyptic illuminations of ancient Babylon, Oriental embroideries, Egyptian secret boxes, silver, gold, and precious stones, the jewelry of kings and queens . . . .'' On and on he spoke, weaving a web of magic around the simple villagers who looked on with wondering eyes. They were all too poor to purchase even a single object. The Assyrian was well aware of their poverty but found great pleasure in presenting his delights, even if only for their eyes. But Joachim, unlike his fellow villagers, *did* possess extra funds. Moving closer to the mer-

73

chant he called out, "Sir, I would like to buy a gift for my daughter. Today is her birthday, and her mother and I want a most special and beautiful gift."

"A gift for a beautiful young girl!" said the Assyrian. "Here is a Chinese gift fit for a queen." He took a large round object, green and blue with spots of brown, from one of the crates and handed it to Joachim. He held the orb in his hands and looked closely at it. It was covered with what appeared to be tiny mountains, oceans and forests. It appeared to be a miniature Earth, yet Joachim knew that the Earth was flat, not round. Suddenly, as if by magic, the globe began to spin in the palm of his hand. "Your daughter would love to play with this beautiful toy," the merchant said. "It would delight a child's heart."

"Yes," agreed Joachim, "she would protect it as she protects and mothers all that she holds in her hands — a kitten, a flower or a bird with a broken wing."

"Or," said the Assyrian, "how about this exquisite doll from India?" He handed Joachim a majestic doll, clothed in regal garments, complete with a golden crown. The glass eyes of the kingly doll appeared to move mysteriously, as if watching one from every angle.

"Ah," thought Joachim, "a perfect gift for Mary." But as he looked more closely at the doll, he saw a defect. The doll's hands and feet had small round holes in them!

The Assyrian merchant saw his puzzlement and said, "No, I don't know why there are holes. The people of India say that the doll is part of an ancient legend of a Cosmic King who will rule heaven and earth, but his hands and feet are pierced."

Joachim shook his head. "No, my Mary would

weep over such a sad little doll. She always takes the pain and suffering of others upon herself."

What a strange doll, what a strange legend, he thought as he handed the doll back to the Assyrian.

"And this most special little girl," asked the Assyrian, "what is her age?"

Joachim beamed with great pride, "Sir, she is twelve this very day."

The traveling merchant smiled a wide and generous smile and said, "Dear sir, I do have wonderful gifts among these treasures, but I am sure that you already know the man who has the *only* gift for your daughter's birthday!"

Joachim cast his eyes to the ground, his heart suddenly saddened, for he knew what the Assyrian meant. But *that* gift was the very one he found so difficult to give her. He slowly nodded assent and thanked the merchant as he made his way out of the circle of wide-eyed villagers who gathered to see the exotic treasures. Slowly, very slowly, as if his sandals were filled with lead, he made his way to the door of the man in the village who possessed the *only* birthday gift for his little girl.

The door opened, and Jacob warmly greeted Joachim, "Shalom, shalom, Joachim, my good neighbor and friend. Ah, you have made the right choice. Yes, yes, come in. Your daughter Mary will be thrilled with your decision. You will make her the happiest girl in all of Nazareth today!"

Joachim nodded agreement and thought, "Jacob and his family are good people." They were not natives of Nazareth but had moved from Bethlehem — a good family in the line of David the King. He knew that Anne would agree with this choice of a birthday gift, even if it was the last gift he wanted to give his daughter. "But," he thought, "Jacob and the Assyrian are right. Even Mary herself would want this gift."

Jacob broke into his thoughts, saying, "The purchase price? It is agreeable?"

Joachim answered softly, "Yes, yes, Jacob, it is agreeable." Then both of them signed the scroll of the purchase contract and shook hands. Joachim walked slowly homeward to Mary and her mother.

Jacob stood in the doorway, holding the scroll and smiling. He unrolled the scroll, allowing the late summer sun to dance across its letters as he read aloud:

JOACHIM AND ANNE OF NAZARETH
DO BETROTH THEIR DAUGHTER MARY
TO JOSEPH OF NAZARETH,
SON OF JACOB AND . . . .

He's gone now, and the day is almost over. I will soon be back in my house with Martha and the children. I have re-read his story here in my journal so I can tell it to my wife. She will love it, I know. At night, sometimes, I tell her the stories I've written down. Some she likes, and some she says she doesn't understand. And when you don't understand a story, it's hard to like it. But that's only because the mind wants instant meaning in everything. Life itself defies such immediate understanding, and I have come to enjoy Igor's weekly stories even if I don't understand all he's trying to say. They're like trips to far-off places. So I just look, taste, feel and try to trust that slowly another part of my mind will unravel the particular meanings that I need now. He told me that the holy books are maps, but I think that his parables are the real maps. I must confess that parts of them

76

are like strange hieroglyphics, and I am able to catch only the more obvious meanings. I look forward to next Saturday.

Saturday, May 17th

Open before me is the gospel of Luke. I like it. I had just finished reading about the visit of Mary to her cousin Elizabeth when there was a knock at my garage door. It was only Igor, being playful. I realize how important his Saturday visits are to me and how much I would miss them if they stopped. I also realize how unpredictable they are. I never know when or if he is coming, but I always go to the garage full of hope and expectation. Today he looked down at what I was reading and one of his five claws touched the line, "My soul magnifies the Lord," and he smiled. "Sent George," he asked, "do you believe that you have a soul?"

"That's difficult to answer," I said. "I'm not sure that I know what a soul is."

He smiled. "Who knows for sure, except perhaps the Maker of Souls? But whatever you call it, that non-material reality within you is nothing to be taken for granted. When you come out here on Saturday, you come to exercise it, to feed it, to push it to the outer limits of its possibilities. What mystics call 'soul power' is a concept we have only begun to grasp. While we have developed our intellectual abilities and extended our physical frontiers, we're stuck in the kindergarten of the spirit. The quest for the Holy Grail, Sent George, is above all a great adventure of the spirit."

A pause followed his remark as we both sat in silence. Over the weeks I had grown comfortable just being in silence. Before, it seemed that something was wrong if I stopped talking. During my times alone on Saturdays, I have grown to enjoy the special bond that links people when they are together in the fullness of silence. It's not a cold silence, when peo-

ple refuse to talk because they are upset or angry, but the full, warm, rich and fertile silence of people who know that words are only one form of communication.

Igor opened a door in our silent communion and asked, "Care to hear a story about souls?"

What could I say but "yes"? I was delighted and eager to hear the story-gift he had brought. I settled comfortably into my chair as Igor began, with a twinkle in his eye.

Once there was a man named Warren Koenig who came home from an estate sale with a bag of various odds and ends. The contents from the drawers of a large walnut bureau, seemingly worthless, had been emptied into a black plastic bag. It was an example of impulse-buying, for Warren, like others, had only glanced inside the bag; but unlike the others, he felt an urge to own whatever was inside.

At home, he carefully removed the contents to see if anything was of value. There was a collection of sea shells, curiously shaped stones, old dog-eared photographs, newspaper clippings, pieces of strangely carved bone and some oily rags. The common thread among these items was that it appeared they all came from Alaska, and the date on the newspaper clippings was 1938.

Unrolling one of the oily rags, he found three small, carved ivory boxes, each no bigger than two inches square. As he turned them slowly in his hand, he recalled that he had seen others like them in a book on American Indians. He knew that all three were "soul-boxes," and by the way they had been wrapped up, it appeared that they had never been used. A rare find it was, indeed!

Several years later he gave the first one away

to his best friend. He opened the small lid, breathed in a part of his soul, and carefully closed the lid. The ritual had been performed with deep devotion and fullness of attention. He waited to see the effect, not knowing how it would feel. He did not feel less, yet he did feel a sense of lightness, a sudden surge of freedom — much like, perhaps, a candle flame that passes on light to another candle. His friend was deeply touched by such a precious gift, and he promised to guard it always with reverence.

He married shortly after that, but for some reason he was unable to give his wife a part of his soul. While he was "madly in love" and their passion and lovemaking was intense, he never told her about his soul-boxes and could never bring himself to give her one. Their marriage lasted seven years and ended in divorce. He was glad that he had trusted his intuition and had kept his secret and his soul.

Later he married again. One night, after they had been married several years, they lay together in bed, an almost-full moon filling the room with a milky light. Full of love, he told her about his Eskimo soul-boxes. That very night, before they fell asleep, he breathed a large part of his soul into the second box and gave it to her. Once again he experienced the sense of lightness and freedom; quietly he fell asleep in her arms, at peace and secure.

As any of his friends would tell you, Warren was a man who was freer than others. There was about him a sense of airiness, even transparency. He was not afraid. He spoke freely, giving his opinions with no concern for the normal need for acceptance or approval — not in a dogmatic manner, but simply as what he believed. He was a free man, unafraid of life, his superiors or even of failure.

One Sunday morning he was at home; his wife had gone to church, and he went to his favorite spot, the small flower garden behind the house. As always, it fed his soul with delight. The small pool of water, the rocks, shrubs and birds all filled him with serenity whenever he stepped into the garden. The roses that grew along the fence he cared for like children.

As he worked in the garden, a large black limousine pulled up in front of his house. A tall man in a dark three-piece suit stepped out of the car; his hair was black, and he had a complexion like lard. He rang the bell and waited, but no one answered. He rang the doorbell a second time and removed an appointment book from his breast pocket. "Hmmm . . . correct address," he said to himself, "and the date, also correct: June 2 . . . time, 10:33 a.m." Still no one came to the door, so he removed a long gold key from his watch pocket and unlocked it. It was a special key that could open *any* locked door, anywhere in the entire world.

The stranger in the three-piece suit walked from room to room but found them empty. In his left hand he held ready a grey velvet bag. Finally, as he stepped through the sliding glass doors onto the patio, he saw Warren asleep in a lawn chair. With a smile on his lips, the stranger walked over and tapped him on the shoulder. But the smile slipped instantly from his lips, for Warren was not asleep — he was dead! "Impossible!" he shouted in rage. "That's simply impossible! The appointment is for 10:33, and it's only 10:31! Yet the body is lifeless — there isn't a trace of soul in him!"

Furiously, the stranger stomped away, swearing that he had been cheated. In his rage, he had failed to notice that in Warren's right hand, as it lay touching the earth, was the handle of a small garden trowel. A few inches away was a small mound of freshly turned earth, no larger than four or five inches in size.

Warren's funeral was attended by many people. In the front pew sat his widow and his best friend. His wife carried a single white rose from Warren's garden. Around the necks of his friend and his wife were small silver chains from which hung white ivory objects. The minister preached away on the familiar theme: "Death comes to us all . . . It is the curse of the sin of Adam . . . Ashes to ashes and dust to dust . . . No one escapes the penalty of death . . . ." Warren's widow and his friend, however, sat smiling through all the funeral service. They knew that Warren, the man they loved, was *not* dead!

"THE SPIRIT WHO IS IN THE
BODY DOES NOT GROW OLD
AND DOES NOT DIE.
NO ONE CAN KILL
THE SPIRIT WHO
IS EVERLASTING."

The Upanishads

SLIDING MECHANISM-
GROOVED TRACK
IN SOUL BOX

He finished the story and took several bites from a peanut butter and mayonnaise sandwich as I reflected on where and to whom I have given parts of my soul. As I thought, he surprised me by saying, "That reminds me, George the Sent, of another story from the beginning of time."

"Another creation story?" I asked in humorous disbelief. "If you ever wrote a holy book, you would never get beyond the first chapter! You're in love with the beginning."

"I know it seems that way," Igor replied, "but that's where it all began. That's where we're all headed, George — you and I and all the wayfarers. As your guide, I need to show you as many maps of the beginning as possible. So, when you get back to the beginning — even if you're in what you think is the middle or the end — you will know that it's the beginning."

Confused but more than ready for two parables on the same day, I nodded consent for us to take off on another adventure. Here is the story he told.

After God had created, with great artistic flair, the earth, the seas, the sun, moon and flowers, it was time to rest. The Divine Artist delighted in all the great and small works of art, but something was missing: the masterpiece needed some movement. So God created birds to fly in the heavens, fish to swim the deep and animals to roam creation. "Nice touch," reflected God, leaning back and taking pleasure in the graceful activity that made the masterpiece come alive, "now it's all finished."

But as time passed, God became bored. The angels began to be concerned with God's listlessness and suggested, "Beloved God, why not take up some hobby to occupy your time?"

God raised a white eyebrow. "A hobby?

Though I enjoy watching a volcano erupting or a tidal wave crashing across one of my seas or even those playful dinosaurs getting stuck in mud pits, I must admit that I *am* bored! Maybe you angels are right — perhaps I *should* take up a hobby to occupy my time since creation is all finished!"

God considered several options — stamp collecting, painting or even building model airplanes — but finally hit upon sculpture. So a visit was paid to the Hobby Shop, and God came back with a huge hunk of clay. Soon the birds and animals began to come to the windows of the studio to watch. A beautiful and awesome figure whose form was like frozen music began to emerge from the divine hands.

As the Divine Sculptor shaped and smoothed the graceful object, an amazing thing happened — God began to fall in love with the clay statue! One evening, after putting away the sculpturing tools, God looked lovingly upon the clay figure, leaned over and kissed the statue on the lips! But the statue did nothing at all. Its eyes were blank and lifeless. God walked home slowly, sad of heart.

When the sun rose the next morning, God leaped out of bed; a marvelous idea had dawned with the sun. God ran down to the seashore, where seaweed and surf merged in the blue-green tides of the ocean. The Divine Being took an enormous breath — Ahhhhhh — filling nose and lungs with the smell of fish and the salty sea. Then God went for a walk in the meadow as the dew glistened diamond-bright on each blade of grass. Standing in a great field of wildflowers, God once again filled both lungs — Ahhhhh — with the aroma of fertile pollen and the exotic beauty of the multicolored blossoms. Leaving the meadow, God climbed to the top of a great mountain, standing knee-deep in white snow. The Creator of All deeply breathed in — Ahhhhhh — the crisp air of the glaciers and the breath and music of the wind as it whistled through the tall ice canyons. Then God raced down the mountain and found a favorite horse. Mounting it and holding on to its flowing mane, God sped off across the rolling prairies like the wind. Racing across the sea of prairie grasses, God was drunk with laughter when the horse stopped at the doorway of the studio. Slipping off the great beast, God hugged the horse, kissed it and breathed in — Ahhhh — the hot, sweaty aroma of the vigorous animal, and then rushed inside the studio.

The Divine Creator stood squarely in front of the lifeless clay statue. God inhaled deeply, then leaned forward and breathed into the silent nostrils. God infused the breath of the sea, the breath of the flowers heavy with pollen, the crisp, sharp breath of the mountain peaks and the hot, sweaty breath of the beloved horse. At the very last, God breathed the divine breath into the still figure, held it close and kissed it with great tenderness.

This time the kiss brought a reaction. The blank eyes opened, and they were full of life. And the perfect body began to move, no longer clay but living flesh. God's greatest masterpiece began to move awkwardly toward the door. As it moved outside, the figure walked faster and faster, then broke into an exuberant run. Wildly it ran through the fields, filling the air with unintelligible shouts. God stood in the doorway, heart pounding with joy and pride.

Circling back, the ex-statue raced to the doorway of the studio. Panting, covered with sweat, the creature stood face to face with God. With lungs rapidly rising and falling, with breath coming in quick spurts, God's newest and greatest creation cried out, "I . . . I . . . I . . . love . . . YOU!"

When I opened my eyes, all I could see was the end of the dragon's long tail as it went through the door. The moon was already up, and the night air was filled with ten thousand perfumes of new life. The smells of May are marvelous, and when they include the aroma of supper drifting out the kitchen window they are beyond counting.

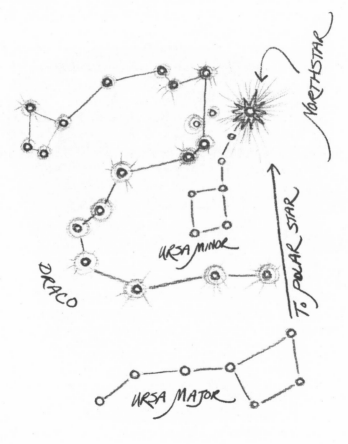

Sunday, May 18th

Last night as I walked across the yard from the garage to the house I felt like a millionaire. Who could be so rich as to walk two tracks, one of the spirit and one of the body, and to have the two as a single pilgrimage? Each time I return from a Saturday in the garage I meet my wife as if for the first time. I love and treasure her more and appreciate how she has so often seen that side of me which I only now see in my hermitage mirror, and yet she still loves me. My children have stopped being burdens and obligations that deny me adventure and have become opportunities to live out what I hear in the dragon's parables.

I stood there last night, my hand on the kitchen door, my heart overflowing like a waterfall. I looked up into the dark and saw, once again, the constellation Draco in the northern sky, and I blew it a kiss: "Thanks, old friend, wherever you are." I have returned here on Sunday morning to jot last night's happenings in my log. May I never forget to be grateful.

Saturday, May 24th

Arrived here shortly after sunrise. Read some, took a nap, sat in silence: nothing! Tried to pray. Nothing! Barren as a closet in a nudist colony. Must I pray for the grace *to pray? Again I feel the frustration of my feeble attempts to communicate with the Divine Mystery. It's a one-way street. I sit here listening and what do I hear? Nothing but my own agitation. There isn't a book on prayer among any of the books Igor gave me, yet everyone in them prays! I need to take some lessons or something . . . .*

"Hi, George," came the salutation, "you look depressed. What's wrong?" I looked at my wristwatch on the table — the time was 4:00 p.m. and it had been a very long and unproductive day.

"You're late," I snapped back, immediately regretting the use of a tone of voice which implied there was an appointed time when he was expected to come. With true grace, Igor did not even acknowledge my rudeness.

"The desert is not always a pleasant place. Our littleness and our inabilities usually come to the surface when we are left alone. As it says in the Tao Te Ching: *'Who can sit still while the mud settles?' Prayer itself can be a hard experience. But put down your frustration for now, and let's travel again on that high road of imagination. Relax, my friend; loosen up, be flexible, and I'll tell you the story of another man who found it difficult to pray.*

This is a story about the Our Father. As all stories seem to, it begins many years ago in happy days. In that time the Our Father lived a comfortable, religious life. He prayed at rosary wakes and was present at both morning and evening prayers. It seemed that he was a perpetual prayer at the times of confessional penance where he usually appeared in sets of three: "Say three Hail Marys and three Our Fathers." He was always an important part of every Mass, whether he was recited or sung. His prayer in Latin rang out strongly, "Pater noster, qui es in caelis . . . ." Secure and comfortable, the Our Father was at peace with his spiritual life. Then came the mid-sixties and its great groundswell of change. During these years he began to experience feelings of doubt about his prayer life. A sense of hollowness and a lack of meaning became like a shadow that followed him each time he went to pray. Whatever the reason, he now began to pray from a sense of obligation. It was his responsibility to pray, but deep within his heart he knew that this could not be a true motive for long. Since at heart he was deeply spiritual, he decided that he must do something about his problem with prayer!

He began by reading books on how to pray. He read articles and attended conferences — but without success. He made a thirty-day Jesuit-directed retreat. While it was an excellent experience, at the end of the thirty days he felt that he still had his problem. Next, he became a member of a Charismatic prayer group. He was baptized in the Spirit and even received the gift of tongues, yet it seemed that his prayer life was incomplete. Since the hollowness remained, he now sought out an Indian guru and became a devoted disciple. Hours on end he would sit in the lotus position and meditate. He stopped eating meat and learned yoga. While feeling a sense of peacefulness in life, he still felt incomplete whenever he went to prayer.

His search for meaning in prayer expanded as he made Marriage Encounter and Cursillo weekends. These also were to no purpose, and his prayer life remained as barren as the Sahara. So in frustration, like so many others, he completely abandoned praying and became involved in social reform. He marched with the Farm Workers, with Women's Rights groups and joined ecologists at sit-ins at nuclear power plants. While doing good and feeling needed, his emptiness at prayer was still part of him. After having tried so many different methods, he finally gave them all up and simply retreated to the Rocky Mountains. There he lived for a year as a solitary hermit in a lonely cabin.

The year of solitude came to an end, and he began his journey on foot down the mountain. He was aware that his problem with prayer, like a shadow, was still with him, and a great sadness filled his heart. Suddenly a thunderstorm broke overhead, and the rain began to descend like a river. Seeking to escape the downpour, he sought shelter in an old mountain cabin. The cabin was perched on a giant rock beside a roaring mountain stream. It was pale grey with age and in the doorway stood an equally aged man. The cabin and the man's clothing indicated that he had not found any gold or silver, but his eyes danced with an inner light that revealed he had found a more valuable treasure. The old man welcomed the drenched stranger into his cabin.

The traveler hung his soaked clothing on the back of a chair that stood by the wood-burning stove, and wrapped himself in a blanket. As he sipped a cup of tea and warmed himself, he decided he would share his story of frustration with the old man. He spoke of his numerous attempts to find a way to pray, his futile trials of various methods and his long months in solitude. At the end of the story, the old man said, "I didn't catch your name, stranger."

"My name is 'Our Father,' although some call me 'The Lord's Prayer.' "

The old man arched his eyebrows like a roller coaster and said, "Why, son, you *are* prayer. You don't have to learn how to pray. You simply have to be who you are!"

And he continued, "I'm a prospector and my trade is to look for gold. But I've learned that there are many kinds of gold. Things like wisdom and truth, as well as those little pieces of yellow rock, are kinds of gold. For the past thirty years I've searched for gold in that mountain stream out there, and I've also searched in those." He pointed to the other end of the cabin. From the floor to the ceiling there were shelves upon shelves of books. There were books of all sizes and shapes. The old man stood up from his chair by the fire and walked over to the book-lined wall. With care he took down a large leather-bound volume with a faded letter "A" on its binding. He carried the book back to the stove and opened it to a certain page. He handed it to the man and said, "Here, read this. Perhaps your problem is not one of method, but something else altogether."

As the rain drummed away on the cabin roof, the weary pilgrim of prayer read, "Aphasia: one of the most serious problems of speech resulting from brain damage or inadequate functioning of the nervous system. This illness shows itself in persons who are unable to speak. The person knows the words he wants to say but cannot negotiate them in speech. Such a person is said to be word-deaf. Aphasia as an illness is caused by an injury to the head. This injury can be a blow or a fall, or perhaps a brain tumor or stroke. The illness can also be congenital." Perplexed, he closed the book and handed it back to the old man.

"*You* are *prayer*," said the old prospector. "You are a special and sacred word of God made flesh. To pronounce your own unique word is to pray the most beautiful and holiest of prayers. You are like the other victims of aphasia. You suffer from the inability to pronounce yourself — to make your own word flesh! Don't feel bad; it is a worldwide sickness and an ancient disease caused by a 'fall.' In you, like all the others, it was passed on at birth."

The old man rose from his chair, poured his guest another cup of tea and continued, "The first word of God made flesh was creation. God said 'sun' and it became flesh — real. And so on with the moon, stars, trees and flowers: they became living prayers. Then God thought a most beautiful thought. God spoke the word and the word became flesh — Adam and Eve. They became God's first human prayers made flesh. But then there came this 'fall,' the original injury that has been passed down from generation to generation. People became unable to pronounce their own word. They were — and they are — word-deaf.

"God doesn't create *things*; God only creates prayers. Men, women, bugs, grass, birds and flowers are created prayers of God. Each is an inspiration of God made flesh or feather or fin. To learn how to pray is not to learn new and poetic words. To learn to pray is to learn to pronounce your own sacred word — to speak yourself! To learn to pray is not to learn a method. It is to know who you are and to be who you are supposed to be. For example, Jesus was a prayerful man not because he prayed but because he *was* a prayer! Jesus was true to the Word that came from his Father, the Word that was himself. In being faithful to who he was supposed to be, he found a cure for the ancient sickness of aphasia. That cure lies in speech therapy — in being true to his word and to your word. Remember, he said, 'Anyone who loves me will be true to my word.'"

There was silence in the old cabin as the traveler thought about what the old man had said. Finally he spoke. "I understand, I think, but how do I cure myself of this aphasia?"

The old man twisted his white beard in his fingertips and said, "First, you must learn to be quiet both outside and inside. There is so much shouting today and so much noise that folks cannot hear their own unique words. Everybody seems to be shouting who you *should* be so loudly that it is difficult to hear your own special word. A million star-years ago, God whispered a sacred and unique word in every soul. It continues to vibrate, but oh, so softly — so softly! Therefore your speech therapy must begin with the therapy of no speech, of silence. For only if you are quiet will you hear the word that resounds within you. You must find quiet places and learn how to be quiet within if you wish to hear your special word.

"The next part of your therapy is learning how to pronounce the word once you hear it. That is the difficult part of the cure, being true to your special personality. You can begin by being grateful for yourself. You must be deeply thankful that you exist and know that the earth is made more beautiful by your presence. This part of the cure is most important. You must see yourself as you are. Everything about the original you is perfect. God does not have bad ideas!"

The old man leaned closer to his guest. His voice was filled with enthusiasm. "What I mean, stranger, is that you must be able to see everything about you as good — your shyness, your intelligence, your creativity, your physical size, the tone of your voice, the shape of your nose and even your baldness. There must be no apologies or regrets. You must not wish to be that word or this word, but totally accept and be grateful for that unique word of God which is flesh in you! This is a most important part of the cure, for unless you can begin to embrace and be thankful for your own word, you can never be true to it. You will keep desiring to be some other word."

Again, there was silence in the small cabin. Outside, the rain seemed to have stopped, but the grey clouds hung low over the tree tops and thunder rumbled on the other side of the mountain. The old prospector rocked slowly in his chair as he watched the face of his guest. Once again the old man began to speak, "If you wish to be true to your word, you will have to be strong. Otherwise you will betray it in the face of the threats and pressures of society. To be true to ourselves and what we should be is perhaps the ultimate responsibility we each bear in life. If God has entrusted you with a creative and unique gift and if it is God's will that you be that special word, then you must summon all the power you have to keep from being forced into the common mold. Speak your own word clearly and with dignity. That is what it means to submit to the will of God. To do God's will and to pronounce your own special word, your own special self, is pure prayer. That is how we 'pray always,' day and night.

"Once you know these things, not with your head but with your heart, you can read any book and it will be a holy book. You can sing any song and it will be a sacred song. For when you are true to your special word, what Jesus said will be true in your life — that he and the Father will come and make their dwelling place with you, always!

Then you don't simply *go* to church, you *are* Church! Then you don't just *receive* the sacraments, you *are* Sacrament!"

With those words the old man grew silent. He closed his eyes and rocked gently in his chair. The rain had stopped, and now the sun fell in yellow ribbons between the dripping branches of the pine trees. The guest rose and began to put on his dried clothing. For a long time he stood before the tall Victorian mirror that hung by the cabin door. He stood in silence looking at himself in the old milk-edged mirror for minutes — or maybe it was for hours. A profound sense of peace and communion with God came upon him. It was a peace that was never to leave him again. Still in front of the old mirror, he began to speak with conviction and profound prayerfulness: "Our Father who art in heaven, hallowed be thy name. Thy kingdom come, thy will be done . . . ."

As he left, the Dragon planted a steam-edged kiss on my cheek. I have to laugh. I had made it such a heavy problem; it now seems so easy, though perhaps living it out will require effort. But at least I now have the solution to work toward. Day has ended, and I feel much better. I will try to trust that all my life is prayer.

"Look within,
Be still,
Be silent...
Know the
stillness of
freedom."

Buddha
The Dhammapda

Saturday, May 31st

I wanted more time here, so I spent last night alone here in the garage. I keep expecting something, yet I wonder if I'm wasting time. It seems so unproductive — all these days, and now a night, in solitude. Nothing to show for my time. No way to evaluate my growth, if there is any. I seem to have lost my way or hit a plateau. Something is going on inside, but I certainly don't seem to be going anywhere. How hard it is to "sit quietly while the mud settles." And this morning I awoke with a sore back and stiff neck. If I'm going to sleep out here, I need something besides a sleeping bag on the floor!

It's mid-morning, and my friend arrived with a bag of doughnuts in a paper sack. I brewed some coffee, and as we ate he told me the story of a man who slept on the ground, as I did last night and old Jacob did in the Bible.

Once upon a time there was a man named Jake who loved to go on camping trips, particularly when he was troubled or needing to think things out. One night Jake went to his favorite spot in the woods and pitched his small, blue nylon tent. After a simple supper, he unrolled his sleeping bag and watched his campfire as it slowly began to die. Overhead, the stars were spread out in a wide swirl of sparkling specks. As Jake was preparing to climb into his sleeping bag, a large dark figure suddenly sprang into the dimness at the rim of the yellow circle of firelight. At the very center of his heart Jake knew that the stranger was God! The two approached each other from opposite sides of the flickering circle, as wrestlers do, bent over and testing each other with their eyes. Jake shouted a challenge: "Your law about marriage is out of date, it needs to be changed! It's too old, God — too oppressive! Thousands of years ago when you gave it to us, young people were engaged at the age of twelve or thirteen. Within a year or two, they were married. The time span between puberty and marriage was brief. Today, Lord, that time span is sometimes ten or fifteen years! Modern life is complex, our life's work or profession is unsure, and people now take on responsibility much later in life. Do you really want your children to spend that many years without love? We need new moral guidelines!"

The tie-up had come, and God and Jake were gripping each other, standing head to head. God, older and more experienced, pulled a leg dive by tackling Jake, and forced him to the ground. God shouted in Jake's ear, "You shall not commit adultery!" With his head pressed hard against the earth, Jake felt the rush of guilt, the heavy weight of centuries of tradition upon him. But Jake was no ordinary wrestler. He grabbed an arm leverage and changed from a defensive position to an offensive one by saying, "Yes, but in the Garden of Eden, you yourself said, 'It is not good for one to be alone.' Right?" Aha . . . now Jake had pinned God's shoulder to the ground. One second, then two, passed; God tried, but couldn't break loose! With a rush of breath, God said, "But how could new guidelines be set for society? What would happen to the institution of marriage? Wouldn't it be weakened if expressions of love outside of marriage were allowed?" Jake still held God's shoulder to the earth, and he shouted in God's ear, "You yourself said that with you, 'nothing is impossible!' With your aid, isn't a new moral concept possible?" Jake's half nelson and crotch hold had pinned God to the ground for three seconds. It was a fall — Jake had contended and prevailed!

God leaped up, standing tall, and said, "Let's go at it again. I'm a little out of practice." Before Jake could respond, God had him in a cross-ankle pickup, and placed full leverage into bringing Jake down hard to the earth. God, with a wide smile, whispered in his ear, "My beloved son, Jesus, said, 'Everyone who divorces his wife and marries another commits adultery.'" With a flip of the divine hand, Jake found himself with his back on the ground. One-half, then a full second passed, as he struggled to free himself.

Then Jake retorted, "Yes, he did say that. But is that a law or a call to perfection? Didn't your son also say that his followers were always to return a blessing instead of a blow for an injury? Was that a call to the perfection of total non-violence, or was it a law? If the words of Jesus are your words, isn't war also a sin? Shouldn't those who support it by taxes, by their silence, by their participation in any way, also be guilty of the sin?"

And so Jake and God wrestled about the rules of responsible parenthood, the evils of consumerism and capital punishment as another form of murder. They wrestled all through the night. First one and then the other was pinned to the earth as they wrestled about the rightness or wrongness of suicide, pollution of the environment, capitalism, nuclear arms, homosexuality, racial discrimination and the role of women in the world and the Church. As the stars slowly turned in their nightly course, God and Jake wrestled together till both were weary.

At daybreak God said, "Let me go, Jake, it's nearly dawn." And Jake released his hold, rose to his feet and limped away wounded. Wounded he was, but not the loser; for, like his namesake of

100

old, he had "contended and prevailed." And God? Well, God did not limp away from the contest, but skipped happily away into the sunrise — for not only was God glad to have had someone to wrestle with again but now there were two or three less of those heavy commandments to carry around all the time!

Finishing his tale, Igor helped himself to the last doughnut in the paper sack. Between bites, he said, "You want to go on a quest, Sent George; that means you must learn to be a wrestler. You need to wrestle with the important questions in your life. You have to wrestle with the self you see in your hermitage mirror, and you must wrestle with God as well. And when you do, know that you will end up as you did this morning — with a sore back and a stiff neck. You can't wrestle God or confront the way you live with what you believe without being wounded, as Jacob was in the Bible. Interesting tale, that one: you see, he was also breaking a law when he crossed the creek to lie down; by trespassing he violated another's legal rights. But the point is that these days, as an entire millenium concludes and another begins, are times of great change. One must face the moral conflicts of the day and continue on an honest quest for the Holy Grail. But I promise you, George, that if you are faithful to your times of silence, you will hear the voice within that calls you to truth. Even if all the rest of the world denies it, you will have the courage to live out what your conscience tells you is truth."

"I'll do my best," I said, "even though I'm not as strong as Jake. Thanks for the surprise of the doughnuts. Will I see you next Saturday?" I asked.

"God willing, Sent George, God willing," he said, and was gone.

Saturday, June 7th

*On the first Saturday in June I sit here sipping the
silence like fine wine. I enjoy these times of being
alone, after the week's demands. As I look back on
the days before I met the dragon, I wonder how I kept
going without these quiet times in my makeshift hermitage. At first my wife objected to our being apart
so often, but then she began to see that when I was
with her, all of me was there. I believe she
understands now that it isn't the amount of time we
spend with each other but the quality that's important. My Saturdays here in the garage have shown
me how to be more present to whatever is happening.
I try to be attentive to each moment, not trying to
do two or three things at once. And I find that my
Saturday lifestyle is becoming a habit; it has carried
over to my work and my family life. I feel that I'm
beginning to understand something, but I'm not exactly sure what it is. It's like dawn before sunrise.
But I do know this: garage time is very important for
me — perhaps it's important for everyone. I recall
reading once about an Assyrian king named
Esarhaddon who threatened his vassals with sixty-
two curses if they didn't treat his son well when he
came to the throne. The curses were varied and color-
ful: that their families would change color like
chameleons, that they would encounter only
murderous women, that they would be caught in
bronze traps. But the last and worst curse was that
they would never again have any privacy. Until my
garage days began, I seemed to have inherited the
last curse of King Esarhaddon. In today's world most
of us have no privacy in our lives . . . . In the midst
of these thoughts, my guru-guide, Igor, arrived.*

"Well," I greeted him, "to what far-off and exotic

land do we travel this Saturday?"

Closing the door behind him with a swing of his long tail, Igor looked down at me and said, "Ah, my young friend, you are eager and ready this morning. I'm glad, for I have a parable that may create a few more reflections in your hermitage looking glass. As you grow in light, you see more. The result is paradoxical. The longer you travel the way of truth, light and holiness, the more sinful you seem! The reason is that you see more, and the light shines back into the dark corners of your consciousness, revealing what usually lies hidden from view."

Suddenly, I was not as excited to hear the parable as I had been. The truth is all right, mind you, but I didn't always find these new views of myself very pleasant. Yet, where can you go but ahead when you've started on a quest? I took a deep breath as Igor began to weave another tale.

One day the Devil came to heaven to visit God. The Devil was upset because the ageless contest between Good and Evil had become an unfair match: Evil did not have the same opportunities as Good. At this most important of all summit conferences, the Devil told God, "I've had a real vocation problem down there ever since Bethlehem when you became incarnate in the world. Since you sent Jesus to live on earth, I've only been able to squeeze in an occasional temptation! By the way, God, that was sneaky of you to choose a stable for his birth. I had my agents posted outside every palace, once we became aware that you were planning an invasion, but you tricked us! Who would have guessed that a God-King would be born in a stable?"

God's face broke into a big grin, like that of a Las Vegas blackjack dealer with all the winning cards in his hand, and said, "All's fair in love and war, my old friend and competitor. But I hate to think of myself as a cheat. Okay, I'll agree to your becoming incarnate in the world also. You're right: ever since Bethlehem I *have* had a slight edge in our contest."

"Great!" said the Devil. "I knew you were a good sport. Now, do I also have the same freedom that you had, to come any time, anywhere and in any form I choose?"

"Only sounds fair," said God. "Any time, anywhere and in any form you choose," and they shook hands on the deal.

And so the Devil, after a quick look around his old home, left heaven and raced like hell for hell, and a meeting with his Ace Demons. As he rushed through the swinging doors, they were jumping up and down, eager to hear what had happened in heaven. "Lord Devil, tell us, tell us, what did the Enemy say?" they shouted.

Wearing a victor's smile, the Devil began, "Well, it was easy. The Enemy agreed that I was right. I've been given complete freedom to become incarnate on the earth in any way I choose."

At this the demons all pounded the table with their fists in fits of uncontrollable glee. The Devil signaled for silence and said, "But now we must put our horned heads together, boys, and figure out the best way for Evil to come to earth! As my advisors, what suggestions do you have?"

"I got an idea," drooled a demon who had white beads of saliva dripping from the corner of his mouth. "Lord Devil, why not come to earth as one of those jasmine-smelling, full-breasted, hot-lipped women of Babylon?"

"What a stupid idea," snapped the Devil. "Too limited. All we'd get would be a few men fooled by lust. No, dummy, we have to find a better

104

disguise — more universal and not so obvious."

For a long time (it's impossible to say how long, since the clocks in hell don't have any hands), the Ace Demons tossed out ideas for the disguise. Some suggested that he come dressed like the god Mars, posing as war. Others suggested that Evil come as money, still others that liquor would be a crafty disguise.

"Shut up, I need time to think," shouted the Devil, as he reached over and turned up the thermostat, causing the big black furnaces to leap into action, sending the temperature up another hundred degrees. And so the Lord Devil and his cronies sat in stalled thought and steaming silence.

"I've got it!" yelled the Devil. "It just came to me. I shall come to earth disguised as the Enemy! Yes, I shall become incarnate in the world as LOVE!" At this all the Ace Demons roared with riotous laughter, as their little tails beat furiously on the scalding steel floors of hell.

Now, if we are honest, we will have to admit that it was a truly ingenious scheme for the Devil to come to earth as Love. For that was how God's son had come and was present in the world at that very moment, even as the best make-up artist in hell was busy transforming the Devil into Love. Actually, the Diabolic Disguise Department provided him with a whole trunk of love disguises.

And so, the Devil came to earth on Valentine's Day, the Feast of Love. He opened up his trunk and took out a disguise. He first put on his red, white and blue suit of LOVE OF COUNTRY. Disguised as "Love of the Father-or-Motherland," he had to work overtime as he busily engaged in war, destruction, lying and spying, brutality, murder, rape and a wide assortment of other vicious deeds. Love of Country made it possible to justify the refusal to forgive, it fed centuries-long resentment and the desire for revenge. It also made possible the blindness to truth that allows evil to flourish in the hearts of people, as the Devil went about singing, "My Country, Right or Wrong . . . ."

Next, the Devil took out the disguise of LOVE OF ONE'S OWN RELIGION. This costume was beautiful in its stained glass colors, heavy with tradition and respectability. Wearing this disguise, it was possible to make people be silent in the face of obvious error and injury. It bred pride and the spirit of superiority — each institution thinking that it was the "one and only." This love also gave permission to hate those of other religions, even to slaughter them in so-called "holy" wars or to ridicule and spread lies about them. The power of this disguise was that it made Love a thing that demanded obedience and unquestioning assent to its teachings, instead of the desire to question or to explore. It was especially effective in the synagogues and streets where Jesus was teaching, as the Devil moved through the crowds whispering, "Heresy — he must be silenced!"

The Devil also wandered over the earth in the form of LOVE OF ONE'S NAME, or SELF-RESPECT. Wearing this form of love, he was able to engage people in murderous duels and fist fights, and other unseemly affairs of "honor" that involved anger, hate, frustration and domination. Another of his incarnations was PARENTAL LOVE. This was a clever mask that made possible the reappearance of one of history's oldest evils, slavery! As Parental Love, the Devil employed sweet, juicy guilt as a tool to let parents control their children even after they were grown. By the use of guilt, parents were able to manipulate and make decisions for their children, making them servants, clones, and vicarious

106

agents for their own needs.

Now, you may have raised an eyebrow when I told you that the Devil became incarnate on Valentine's Day. That you should be surprised should not surprise you! In fact, before the Devil left hell, one of the Ace Demons questioned him: "Lord Devil, *why* are you coming to earth as Love? I suspect that you have another reason, other than to come disguised as the Enemy."

"Ah," said the Devil, "you're a clever little demon. Yes, you're right. I have a very good reason: Love makes people blind! If Evil comes as Love, I can blind them to the reality of what is happening. They will become 'a people living in darkness.' I have chosen Valentine's Day because it is their Feast of Love. While I can sell evil under the form of Love of Country or Religion, under the disguise of Love of One's Name, or even Parental Love, the more clever ones will see through my disguises. But who will ever suspect me as LOVE FOR ONE ANOTHER?"

And so, as Love For One Another, Evil introduced domination, control and the exploitation of others. While ordinarily kind people would never think of stealing money, Love allowed them to steal affection, time, pleasure, body and soul — and never really to share themselves. Under the disguise of Love, one person could "own" others, keeping them from loving anyone else by giving or refusing affection. Pain could be inflicted by words, suspicions, by refusal to forgive or by the ugly use of silence. People who never lied could be easily led to use lies like, "I love you . . . I will always love you . . . ," without ever backing up such words with commitment. And the people who were being injured by this disguised love? They themselves participated; they were silent when they should have spoken. They allowed exploitation and did nothing. They reacted out of guilt and did not rebel . . . all because of "Love"! Oh yes, under these forms of Love, Evil was able to dwell in every home and heart. The Devil was so right: earth-people *did* become "a people living in darkness."

At halftime, the contest between Good and Evil seemed to be over! The Devil was winning with such overwhelming odds that his victory seemed certain. So the Devil sent God a message, asking if Good wanted to "toss in the towel" and concede defeat. Now it was God and his angels who sat in silence, pondering the questions, "How do we lift the darkness? How do we dispel the blinding gloom, so that people can see the difference between God as Love and the Devil as Love?"

Finally, after much reflection, God spoke slowly, "I know a way to make my children see the difference. But oh, how I hate to use it. It pains my heart to even consider such a solution, but I know no other way. The Light must break loose, or else the world will be truly lost to Evil. I shall ask my son, Jesus, to show them the difference."

And so, on a certain Friday in spring, Jesus died on a cross on a barren hilltop in Palestine. At that moment a light flooded the world, so intense that no one could mistake the difference between real love, and Evil disguised as Love. The cross revealed the enormous difference between the two: real love gives unconditionally, while counterfeit love takes. Authentic love gives freedom; imitation love, on the contrary, enslaves and attempts to own the other. Genuine love is expansive, is ever out-reaching, while love as a forgery is a closed circle, restricted and exclusive, allowing no room for others. Godly love is humble, generous and honest, while evil love is proud and self-seeking and basically dishonest. All this the death of Christ made clear in a blazing revelation. It was not on Christmas that the Light entered the world. No, it was on Good Friday, the Feast of the Revelation of True Love. On that Black Friday, a people who lived in blindness, in darkness, saw a great light — and it revealed *true love* forever!

So, even to this day, those who are uncertain if their love is real or only a counterfeit can illuminate the darkness of doubt by holding up their love to the eternal sign of the cross.

When he had finished, I didn't need to hold up my hermitage mirror. I could see clearly how I have used love as a weapon, as a tool to get what I want. But the parable also gives me courage to try to love in a different way, in the way the Mystery loves me and the world. What I feel at the close of this day is not guilt but a challenge. I have often loved selfishly, but now I so want to love without thinking of myself. We shall see what happens in the future.

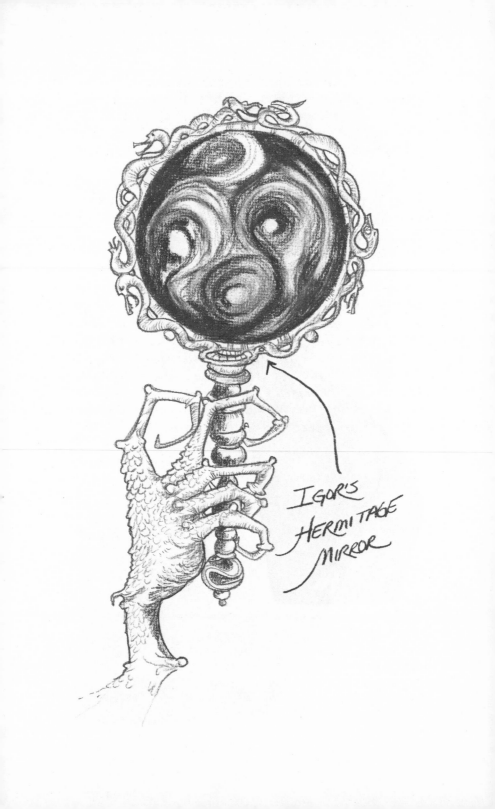

IGOR'S
HERMITAGE
MIRROR

Saturday, June 14th

This morning my kids asked me what I wanted for Father's Day. It's interesting that there's a holiday to help you remember your father! God, who is beyond image or name, was seen by Jesus as a loving and compassionate father. Have I been such a father? Is the divine title of "Father" merely the result of human invention . . .? As I paced around my hermitage asking myself these questions, my Saturday visitor arrived. I knew he was near, because I smelled that unique aroma of the Fourth of July, the distinctive odor of fireworks and rockets.

"Good morning, George," he greeted me. "I hope you have your traveling boots on, for this Saturday we are going back into pre-history!"

"To the beginning again? Do you have another story about the creation of the world?" I asked, all set for another swing around Genesis.

"No, not that far, my friend," Igor replied, "but back a long, long way. Today we'll journey to Paleolithic times, to the days of cavemen and cavewomen, for a tale that I think you will find interesting." I had to smile, for I had found all his fantastic tales challenging and interesting — though sometimes very puzzling!

"Please begin, faithful companion of the Quest," I said playfully. "Take me to the places I need to go. Lead me to the horizons I can't reach alone."

"Now, that's the spirit!" replied Igor. "Close your eyes and let the magic theater of your mind take you back into the wonderland of imagination . . . .

Long, long ago, perhaps twenty thousand years ago, there lived a tribe of people who clustered in caves on a ridge overlooking a vast, rolling prairie. The women were the first of the tribe to become aware that a divine force was active in their lives. They saw the power as a source of life and fertility. They bowed down before crude images of this fertile power in the form of a woman's body with great hips and generous breasts. First the children and then the men of the tribe also began to worship this Mother Goddess, the ruler of life and nature. Woman shamans had served this Great Mother, but of late they had been replaced by men as the spirit leaders of the tribe. The women shamans were given the task of gathering special herbs and being healers, as the men shamans exercised spiritual power in the clan.

At that time no distinctive name had yet been invented for fathers. Men were divided between those with a mate, called "Guardians of the Clan," and those unmarried, who were called "Young Ones." One day, the Guardians and the Young Ones gathered to hear the words of the chief of the cave. "We will never be the strongest of all the tribes as long as babies come only from women's bodies and are raised by the women. We need a new magic to grow fighting men." Then, looking directly at the shaman, he continued, "You must give us the magic that women have so that we also can have babies! Then we will raise the strongest men in all the world."

At this the men shouted in agreement, their faces bright with promise as they sat encircling the fire. Now keep in mind that this was long, long ago and the rules of biology were unknown. The marvel of life was thought to be a gift from the Goddess and the result of magical spells. So the shaman went off into solitude for three days and nights.

When he returned, he delighted the men by

giving them the magic of having a baby. The tribal leaders decided they must proceed slowly, lest they offend the Mother Goddess. So only one man, the strongest warrior of all the tribe, was selected to be the first to bear a child. Nine months later, he bore a son.

The boy child was reared only by the men and soon grew to be the strongest fighter and the fastest runner. The men began to dream of becoming the greatest tribe on earth. But this man who came from a man's body was not only the greatest warrior, he was also cruel beyond imagination. He delighted in killing, even when there was no need for food or self-protection. His viciousness exceeded that of any beast. The weak and the aged, as well as the enemy, were frequently victims of his brutality.

The elders of the tribe could see that his presence was destructive to the good of all, and so he was driven away into the vast flatlands that rolled unceasingly westward from their caves in the cliffs. The experiment had been a terrible disaster. But that did not stop the men from wishing to be the strongest of all warriors.

Again a meeting of all the men and their shaman was called. This time they insisted, "Why must we worship a woman-god? We want a god who is like us — a man-god!" When the warriors demanded a new god, some of the men were frightened that evil would befall them if they banished the She-God, who had been their only god as long as anyone could remember. But the warriors were insistent, and so the shaman once again went to the sacred cave.

Alone, deep in the earth, in the bowels of the mountain, the shaman looked at the mystical markings on the cave's walls, the spirals and circles carved in the stone. In this place where only shamans were allowed, the holy of holies where the She-God dwelt, the shaman bowed his head to the floor and prayed. "O Great and Holy One, once again the men have sent me to you for magic. Now they want a man-god, a new god who will be like them. What am I to do?"

Directly in front of him was a gaping hole in the cave wall, faintly illumined by the light from a tiny wick floating in a crude stone bowl filled with animal fat. The sound of the wind could be heard as it howled up and down the narrow, twisting shafts that honeycombed the mountain. As the wind swirled from the sacred hole, the tiny flame jumped fitfully, causing the yellow shadows on the cave walls to flicker and tremble. Out of the dark opening a voice spoke. "We know, don't we, my beloved one, that I am neither man nor woman! It matters little to me what they call me or what images they make of me as long as they worship *me* and not themselves! But you, my little one, my beloved shaman, do you not fear what will happen if you give them their man-god? Did they not learn from their last gift of magic that harmony requires balance?"

The shaman, his forehead pressed tightly against the damp cave floor, murmured in agreement. Slowly he raised his face fearfully to the sacred opening. "Yes, Great One, I also fear that if they have a man-god they will make him a warrior god! Then they will grow to enjoy cruelty and killing. The sickness will spread to all the tribes until the earth herself will be in great peril. But they demand that I bring back the magic. What am I to do? Is it possible that you, O Great One, can find a way to keep the new magic from leading us to destruction and evil?"

Again the whistling wind filled the twisting shafts; then all was silence. The silence grew and

114

grew until it thundered in the ears of the shaman-priest. God had spoken. A cold draft blew sharply from the sacred hole and consumed the tiny flame of the oil lamp in one great bite. All was darkness. The sacred encounter deep in the mountain was ended. Slowly the shaman rose to his feet and left the sacred sanctuary.

As he came out of the holy cave, all the men of the tribe rushed to surround him. The sun, a massive, scarlet ball of fire, paused briefly on the western horizon as if it also wished to hear what message the shaman carried from the depths of the earth. With a strong voice, the shaman spoke. "The She-God is dead! The new god of this tribe is a man-god. He will dynamically reshape this tribe and all the earth. He has given me a new word for our language — his name. God wishes to be called 'Father.' " The men slowly repeated the strange new name as excitement and pride filled their hearts. The shaman continued, "This new name, 'Father,' means 'He who loves constantly and defends the weak and sick — who loves peace and order — who allows all things to be as they were created.' But most of all, this name means 'Great Love.' " In awe and wonder the men repeated slowly the new divine name, "Fa . . . Fa . . . Father!"

The shaman held his hand high for silence, saying, "There is more magic! He desires that each one of you who is the head of a clan shall bear his holy name."

At this the men were stunned in wonder. "Yes," continued the shaman, "each of you is to be his priest-father in your own clan. You are to be called 'father' by your children. You are to be like clear, quiet pools of water that reflect what looks into them; you are to be reflections of our Father-God."

And the sun, the single, scarlet sky-eye, which had paused to listen to the message as it stood at the edge of the world, began to descend again into the womb of the night. As it disappeared beneath the horizon, the old shaman smiled and spoke softly, "Good night, O sun. Some day you will rise on that most special day when God will share the greatest secret of the cosmos with the children of the earth: God's *real name*."

Since it was late spring and the daylight hours were longer, it was still light when he finished the parable. The sun was only at the tree tops, but the magic of his story wasn't lost. We sat in silence as I wondered if my love for my family is divine. To be godlike requires so much energy. It takes you to the absolute limits of what is possible. But perhaps that's when the God-seed inside you explodes, when you push yourself beyond the possible to what is impossible. It's like breaking the time barrier, when suddenly you find that you have leaped into another dimension.

I was so lost in my thoughts that I failed to notice that Igor had silently slipped out the door. I was alone — and yet I was not alone. My friend is more than a teacher; he stays with me somewhere inside as I try to put into practice what I learn in the back of the garage. As I conclude this hermitage day, I thank God for the gift of the dragon and for the unexplainable invitation to set out on the quest for the Holy Grail.

"I AM THE FATHER
OF THIS UNIVERSE,
THE MOTHER,
THE SOURCE,
THE INEXHAUSTIBLE
SEED.

I AM THAT
WHICH IS AND
THAT WHICH IS
NOT..."

Bhagavad gita

Saturday, June 21st

I see that my last entry talks about the quest for the Holy Grail. I wonder when I will be ready to set off with the dragon to begin the search. Week after week I have come to my garage. I have fasted, prayed and spent time in solitude. I have studied the great holy books and puzzled over the maps of the parables. Surely, I will be ready to leave soon. What more is necessary?

I had hardly finished entering this last sentence in my log when I heard a loud thump on the roof of the garage. Slowly the smiling face of Igor appeared over the edge of the roof. "Sorry, I overshot the yard — had to land on the roof or I would have crashed into your neighbor's patio, and that would have caused a big fuss, not to mention a lot of explaining!" With the agility of a teenager, he swung his great scaled body over the edge of the garage and dropped with a plop on the lawn.

"I love summer!" he began as he entered, carefully coiling his tail in the corner. "The air is great for flying! I've never been much of a winter creature. Dragons and ice and snow just don't go together, if you know what I mean."

I had opened the windows of the garage and it wasn't too hot yet, but I wondered what it would be like in the afternoon. I was sure that the dragon wouldn't notice, but I hoped for my sake that he would control his fiery breath. Since I had been laboring over it all week, the first thing I asked was when we would be able to start our expedition.

He leaned back against the wall and smiled. "Patience, my young friend, you must be patient. All these things take time. You surely must have read in the holy books that conversion is the first stage

118

of any successful quest. Conversion is nothing more than a personal revolution. Less than a month from now, on the Fourth of July, you'll celebrate the revolution of your country. Since early March, you personally have been involved in an ongoing revolution in attitude and lifestyle. But keep in mind that such conversion must continually happen. We so easily excuse ourselves of that need for constant reform. Take the case of Nineveh, the rich man in Jesus' story-parable about the poor beggar Lazarus . . . .

His lips were cracked with thirst, a thirst so great that poor Nineveh could have drunk the Mississippi dry without a pause. Day after day he shouted across the great abyss that separated the blessed from the damned, pleading with Father Abraham to grant him just one wish.

Once Nineveh had worn precious Egyptian linen undergarments and regal purple robes from Tyre as he and his numerous guests dined on the choicest food, wiping their greasy hands on bread and throwing those whole-wheat napkins to the dogs beneath the table. To him had belonged the rewards of those who work hard and succeed greatly — luxury, rich food and fine wine. But now his beautiful purple vestments were ruined by the brimstone smoke and fire of hell. His once-corpulent flesh hung in overlapping folds from his rickety bones, and his gold rings had slipped off his skinny fingers. In dramatic contrast, Lazarus, who had once begged pitifully at his front door, now reclined in the bosom of Father Abraham, enjoying all the eternal delights of paradise. Death had reversed the roles in the courts of the blessed across the great abyss, and Nineveh had become the beggar. Day after day he called across the dark bottomless chasm, "Please, oh please, Father

Abraham, grant me just *one* favor!"

Finally, after months of celestial time had passed, weary of his constant begging, Father Abraham finally relented and said, "Alright, alright — what do you want?"

"One small favor, Father Abraham," Nineveh pleaded hoarsely. "I don't ask that Lazarus should leave the pleasures of your bosom; I only beg that you should allow me to go to my five brothers and call them to repentance."

Father Abraham shouted back, "I will have to speak to Yahweh. You know they have rules around here about that sort of thing!" So days passed, and weeks and months, and all the while poor Nineveh longed for one drink of cool water as the fires of hell turned his skin to brown parchment. His anxiety about the fate of his brothers increased as his own misery grew.

Finally, after months of waiting, Father Abraham shouted across the deep abyss, "The Lord God, blessed be the Holy One who is Pure Mercy, has decided that you may return to your brothers. But there is one condition. You will be allowed to speak only four words to them — and those four words must come from Moses or the prophets!"

"What?" said Nineveh. "Only *four* words? How can I warn them if I am only allowed to speak four words?" The once-rich man, while delighted with permission to return to the world of the living, was beside himself with anxiety. How would he ever be able to condense his warning into four words — and those not even his own? And what *had* Moses and the prophets said?

Now in the pits of hell, unlike the ordinary hotel or motel, there are no bibles! So Nineveh tried to remember all the readings he had heard from the prophets when, out of dutiful piety, he had attended the synagogue. He forgot the fires of hell, the eye-smarting smoke and the constant ear-shattering noise, which was even worse than the heat, as he tried to find the right four words.

As he reflected upon his sins with ever-growing understanding, the words of the prophet Amos resounded in his ears. "Woe to the complacent in Zion! Lying upon beds of ivory, stretched comfortably on their couches . . . ."

"Yes," he thought to himself, "I will take the first four words. These I will speak to my brothers. It was my complacency, my satisfaction with myself, which blinded me to the needs of Lazarus and all the poor."

And so, with his divine passport, Nineveh left hell and returned to earth. He chose to visit his youngest brother first. He was a plain young man who had always worked the family farm. When Nineveh arrived, his brother was plowing a field with his jackass, Geraldine.

Not knowing how to materialize in an unobtrusive way, Nineveh suddenly appeared before his startled brother in the middle of his field. "Whoa, Geraldine," shouted his brother to the jackass. And the jackass stopped dead in its tracks as the ghostly Nineveh stood with arms upraised. "Woe to the complacent!" he cried out, his voice filled with pleading.

"Whoa, *whoa* . . .? How *can* I stop? Whoever you are, you talk just like my wife. She's always telling me to slow down, to take time. Who can take time when the fall planting is to be done, the fields to be turned over, the seeds planted? Stop to talk to my son or to her? Stop to visit about trivial things when there's *work* to be done? Soon winter will be here. There'll surely be time to talk then. Whoa to the complacent indeed! Be realistic!"

Poor Nineveh! All he could say were his four words, so he repeated them, his voice vibrant with compassion and urgency, "Woe to the complacent!" With that his brother picked up a clod from the ground and threw it over the jackass' head toward the grey shadowy image standing in front of him. "Giddyap, Geraldine, we got work to do! I don't understand. I do my best to be a good husband and father to my family. What more can I do? I can't be in two places at once. I try to run a successful farm, manage my affairs, put food on the table and what do I get at home — and now here in the field? Sermons about doing *more*!" And he and Geraldine plowed on into the sunset.

A miserable failure with his first brother, Nineveh moved on to the next, who was a successful and respected businessman, a pillar of his synagogue. As an outstanding citizen of his village, he had been selected for the "Most Generous Citizen" Award three times.

It was late at night when Nineveh arrived at his brother's house. His brother had just come home from a long meeting of the Concerned Citizens Committee. He had slipped into a soft silk bathrobe and pushed his feet into his fur-lined slippers. On his stereo was a new album, Billy Squire's *Emotions in Motion*. Billy himself was belting out the lyrics, "You got a lot to learn, you play with fire and you might get burned ... Learn how to give, learn how to take, before it's too late ...." He had settled into his leather recliner with a glass of Cabernet Sauvignon when Nineveh stood before him, wearing his tattered, faded purple robes. With upraised finger, Nineveh spoke with great feeling, "Woe to the complacent!"

"What or who are you?" gasped his brother, spilling his wine on the floor. "You look like my deceased brother, God be good to him. But what is this strange message, 'Woe to the complacent'? Daily I labor to assist the poor and needy. I sit on twelve committees to care for social needs. My day is filled with meetings for the public good. I'm so busy I don't have time even to pray . . . thank God that charity is prayer. Who are you — phantom, ghost or a spirit of the devil? My brother Nineveh was a good man, respected by all — a success in every way, good to his friends and family. If any man deserves the rewards of the blessed, it is my brother. And if God should choose to send him to me, I am sure he would say, 'Congratulations, brother. Keep up the good work!' Certainly he would have no reason to say something silly like 'Woe to the complacent!' How could I do *more*? What more could God expect from me?" And with that, he threw a pillow at his brother Nineveh saying, "Away from me, you illusion, you spectre of hell!"

And so, shaking his head, poor Nineveh departed. "Surely," he thought to himself, "I am not to fail entirely. Perhaps my brother Samuel will listen. Of all my brothers he is the most devout, a man of prayer."

Nineveh did not go to his brother's house, but went instead directly to the temple, for he knew that his brother prayed three times a day. Arriving in the sanctuary, he found Samuel with his arms uplifted in prayer. He tapped him on the shoulder and stood before him, gaunt finger raised skyward, and spoke his message: "Woe to the complacent!"

His brother opened his eyes and said, "Amos, chapter 6, verse 1. One of the more beautiful sayings of that prophet, who lived, probably, from 786 to 746 B.C., during the reign of King Jeroboam. Not a professional prophet, mind you, but still a holy man!"

Again Nineveh cried, "Woe to the complacent!" And again he repeated it, his voice trembling with anxiety and concern.

"Amos spoke to a troubled time," responded Samuel, oblivious to the presence of his brother standing before him, "the threat of pestilence, blight and all those woeful things; the repudiation of shallow worship and lip service. Thank the Lord we now have this beautiful temple, these lovely, comforting ceremonies and our sacramental prayers. Keep the laws, mind the observances of Moses, keep the Sabbath holy . . . do these and heaven is yours. Praise the Lord for his salvation! Praise the Lord, Alleluia!"

He was still reciting praises to himself as Nineveh left the temple in despair. "Why," he thought, "should I even bother to go to my other two brothers? It will be just the same. They do not want to hear anything that will cause them to question their well-worn patterns or challenge them to change or search for the real values in life. Father Abraham was right: even if someone returns from the dead, even from hell itself, they will not listen if it is not what they expect to hear. Their lives, even their prayers, are cast in the stone of habit."

And so, that night, the despairing Nineveh slunk back into hell. The fires roared as the smoke billowed up, and the noise blared louder than ever. As he remembered his former life of luxury, he could agree with Dante: "There is no greater sorrow than to be mindful of the happy times in misery." But he would add, "A greater sorrow is to have tried to warn those you love against calamity and know that they have not heard."

The next morning, as the lamentations and loud wailings resounded through the sunless smoke, and voices hoarse from pleading begged

124

for a single drop of water, a strange thing happened. A band of angels belonging to the Heavenly Corps of Engineers began to erect a pontoon bridge across the great abyss between paradise and hell. Nineveh, together with the other damned, watched with great curiosity. "Perhaps," they said to each other, "another Lucifer or more fallen angels are to join us."

But that was not the case. As Nineveh stood watching in the murky haze, he suddenly recognized the bright figure of the beggar Lazarus hurriedly approaching him over the precarious causeway. "Come quickly, Nineveh," he cried. "Come, cross the bridge quickly; we have only a few moments. You must not delay!"

"What?" said Nineveh in total disbelief. "Why should I, a sinner, be allowed to come to the bosom of Abraham?"

With a short but fervent embrace Lazarus smiled and said, as he began to lead him across the temporary bridge, "Because, dear man, you were given one wish, but you did not ask anything for yourself, not even a drop of water. Your only concern was that you might help others. Even though they did not hear and repent, you have found your own salvation in forgetting yourself. Billy Squire's song says it all: 'Learn how to give, learn how to take . . . .' Nineveh, you've learned! Come now and join me in the bosom of Abraham!"

The dragon's parable had opened several doors in my mind. As I was considering which of them to explore, he surprised me by saying, "Tuck that parable away and think about it later; I have one more for you today about another kind of conversion . . . .

125

His name was Reverend Sam. He wore a black suit, a white shirt with a black shoe-string tie and black cowboy boots. He drove a battered school bus that had been painted bright white. On top of the bus was a large cross, flanked by two flapping American flags; from behind them two large trumpet-shaped loudspeakers blared out old-time gospel music. Half of the bus was filled with give-away bibles and the other half was the makeshift home of Reverend Sam. Painted in large red letters on either side of the bus were signs that read: BAN E.R.A., GAY RIGHTS AND COMMUNISM—BUT NOT THE BOMB! and REPENT AND BELIEVE THE GOOD NEWS. Across the front was JESUS IS LORD, and the back carried the slogan GOD BLESS AMERICA, FIRST!

As the Reverend Sam drove along, both hands gripping the steering wheel, his voice raised to accompany the taped *Amazing Grace* blasting from the speakers, he saw a hitchhiker ahead at the side of the road. He was a man in his late twenties or early thirties with a dark beard, old clothes and a tattered backpack.

The Reverend Sam slammed on the brakes, and the Bible Bus came to a grinding stop. He flung open the door with a zestful "Praise the Lord!"

The hitchhiker looked up, smiled and said, "Good morning. Beautiful day, isn't it?"

"Climb aboard, stranger," replied the Reverend Sam. "I'm headed up the road as far as the turnoff for Circleville. You might as well ride that far."

The hitchhiker climbed into the seat beside Reverend Sam as he shifted gears, causing the old bus to lumber off with a medley of mechanical moans. Turning down the volume of *Amazing Grace*, the Reverend Sam asked with a big grin,

"Have you, stranger, accepted Jesus as your personal Lord?"

At first the hitchhiker didn't answer. Then he said in a quiet voice, "As Lord? You mean *my* Lord? No, I don't think I have."

"But stranger," said the Reverend Sam with an expression of shocked disbelief, "you will never be saved unless you do! That's my whole life — bringing folks to the love of Jesus, baptizing them and spreading the bible far and wide. That's why I'm headed for Circleville — to preach a revival."

The hitchhiker smiled and said nothing. The Reverend Sam, lowering his head and looking over the top of his glasses just as Lyndon Johnson used to do, asked, "Have you been baptized in the name of the Father, and of the Son, and of the Holy Ghost?"

Again, a long silent pause. The hitchhiker finally answered, "No, come to think of it. I just never thought it was, ah . . . necessary."

"What?" exclaimed the Reverend Sam. "Do you mean that you don't belong to a Church?"

"Do you mean," asked the hitchhiker, "to *one* Church?"

"Yes, of course," said the Reverend Sam. "How can anyone belong to more than one Church? The truth is one. Either you believe or you don't. If you believe, as I am sure you must, then you can be baptized and saved." The lips of the Reverend Sam parted in a slight smile as he thought to himself, "I got myself a real, live, genu-wine heathen, ready for the waters of redemption!"

The Reverend Sam was a salvation salesman of the first order. He now rested his heavy hand on the arm of the hitchhiker and began a long, convincing sales talk on the necessity — the absolute necessity — of being baptized.

Up ahead was a sign to the right that read

"Circleville, 10 Miles," pointing to a narrow road. Winding alongside the main road was a clear-water creek.

Pulling the old bus to the shoulder of the road, the Reverend Sam took the stranger by the arm and marched him down to the creek. There he submerged him under the clear, flowing waters and cried aloud, "I baptize you in the name of the Father, and of the Son, and of the Holy Ghost." As the hitchhiker moved out of the water, the Reverend Sam shouted a loud victory cry that was a rare combination of Alleluia, Yippie and Hooray!

Then the Reverend Sam warmly wrapped his arm around the wet shoulders of the silent hitch-hiker and led him back up the road without ever really looking at him. Then he climbed alone into the bus and said, "Here's where we part company, brother." He handed the stranger a bible and closed the door, shouting, "Praise the Lord." The old, white Bible Bus, with banners flapping, roared off in a great grey cloud heavy with oil and gas fumes.

As he started up the narrow road that led to Circleville, the Reverend Sam wore a smile that translated, "Mission accomplished." He looked into his rearview mirror for one last glimpse of his most recent convert.

But, in his mirror he could clearly see that the intersection of the two roads was empty. No one could be seen anywhere.

"What a strange story," I said when he had finished. "It's like the Emmaus story turned inside out. The Reverend Sam was too busy preaching to see who the stranger really was!"

"Yes," Igor replied, "and I have a feeling that it is repeated more often than you or I might think."

As the twilight of that June evening enveloped the garage, I was suffering from overdose. Truly I needed time to sort out what these parables mean for me. Sensing my need to think, Igor bowed and slipped out the door without another word.

Those two stories do puzzle me. In the first parable Nineveh got rewarded for trying to change his brothers' lives, even though they didn't listen. But in the other one, it seemed wrong for the Reverend Sam to preach at the hitchhiker the way he did. What's the difference between them? Was the Reverend Sam just collecting souls? Doesn't love have to be at the heart of all conversion?

"You SHALL LOVE THE LORD
  Your GOD
WITH ALL your HEART
WITH ALL your SOUL
WITH ALL your STRENGTH
AND WITH ALL your MIND
AND your NEIGHBOR
AS Yourself."

Jesus
The Gospel of Luke

Saturday, June 28th

I've been thinking about conversion all week. If conversion means change, it certainly has happened to me. Six months ago I wouldn't have dreamed I'd be spending every Saturday in solitude and silence. Indeed, if there is such a thing as positive addiction, then I am addicted to these times of quiet. And I have grown to need the weekly visits of my friend Igor as much as I need food or rest. Over the months I have come to enjoy and accept his presence in my life as normal — as if having a dragon for a friend were the common thing. It only seems strange when I'm in the hurry-hurry world of day-to-day life. My friend is more real to me than much of what I have taken to be reality. I value deeply our friendship, founded on our mutual search for Truth. Each Saturday night when I say farewell to him, I fear that one of these nights will be the last time. That apprehension has grown, day by day, into an abiding sense that something is going to happen soon. I make note of that only because I have tried to be honest with myself in all that I have written here.

The month of June will soon be over. How quickly time slips by! Ever since Igor began his visits, though, I have not felt that I am wasting time, no matter how fast it passes. For once in my life, each day has taken on a sense of supreme importance. Eternity has become more real for me. A kind of timelessness seems to be breaking more and more into the clock-counting world that I inhabit.

It was hot today, and I had all the windows open as I sat in my shorts enjoying the caress of summer. Above the roar of my neighbor's lawn mower I heard a "Psst . . ." and looked up to see the face of my friend filling the front window of my hermitage. "May I in-

terrupt your thoughts?" Igor asked with his usual smile.

"Come in, old buddy," I said, delighted to see him. "I had hoped you might stop by today, but I wasn't sure."

"Yes, George, we're never sure about anything, if we're honest. Who knows how long any friendship will last on this level? But all true friendships are eternal." Although his presence in my makeshift hermitage caused the temperature to go up at least twenty degrees, I didn't mind. It was so good to see him again!

"I was passing by," he said, still smiling, "and thought I might drop in and see how you were."

"Oh, fine, just fine," I answered. "Anxious, of course, for us to pick a date for the quest to begin. I think that I'm about ready, don't you? I will need to make some arrangements, you know, for time off at work and to let my family know that I am leaving." As I talked on, he nodded his head in agreement, but I felt that something was missing. Affirmation or enthusiasm were not in his eyes, in his presence. Again I became deeply aware that our times together are limited. With a stiff arm I pushed the thought back into the dark swamp of my unconscious as I asked, "Well, to what far distant and exciting land do we venture on this Saturday?"

The invitation to tell a tale caused his eyes to sparkle. "Ah, yes," he said, "time for a parable. But this time, my friend, it won't be from the beginning or from far away. This story is hidden in this very room!" He pointed to the corner where I had hastily stacked a tall pile of old Time magazines. I walked over and began to dig through the pile as he directed me. "No, not that one. No, further down — I believe that the date is 1982. Look for the March 1 issue."

I continued my search in the dusty pile until I found the magazine he wanted. "Now," he said, *"turn to the art section on page seventy and read the article."*

It was about a show of folk art at the Corcoran Gallery in Washington, D.C. Robert Hughes, the Time *writer who had covered the art show, spoke about a special piece — a throne built for God by a black janitor named James Hampton. His creation, intended not so much as a work of art but as a work of worship, was called "The Throne of the Third Heaven of the Nations Millenium General Assembly."*

Hampton was both a folk artist and a unique sort of religious prophet. What made him unique was that he founded his own personal religion — and was its sole member! Hampton believed that God and other heavenly visitors spoke to him each night in his garage. God whispered to him, and he was visited in his nightly work by Moses, the Virgin Mother of God and even Adam. His old brick garage in Washington, D.C. was a new Mount Sinai, a Jerusalem and a Garden of Eden. Time and space had telescoped into one. When I read that, I looked up at my friend in surprise. He only smiled and indicated that I should continue reading.

The message Hampton heard was that the end is near and that he should build a throne for God and all the heavenly company. Over the years Hampton had painstakingly constructed what was to be a sanctuary for the end of history. He had built over 180 pieces of sanctuary furniture for angels and saints to use at the Second Coming. Nowhere on any of his 180 pieces was there an image of an angel, a saint or even of Jesus. All the furniture for the Assembly was an empty stage awaiting the Blessed Ones who would use it.

As I read on, my wonderment grew, for James Hampton had constructed the entire creation for the end of time not out of marble or gold — but out of

132

junk! The Throne of the Lord Yahweh was made from trash, old paper, aluminum and metal foil. At his death in 1964, his sanctuary was unfinished but breathtaking in its beauty.

I put the magazine down, and fear joined us as a third party. What was my mentor saying? Was I to experience what James Hampton had? I silently looked for an answer, but he only looked deeply inside me. He acknowledged my fear but did not address it. Time and space had telescoped for James Hampton in his garage, and they surely had, at this moment, for me.

Like Hampton, I too have heard God in my garage. Like him I have told no one. Who would believe me? Indeed, the Gospels tell us, "Be watchful, stay awake . . . be prayerful, you know not the appointed time." True, but God coming in a garage?

Igor finally spoke. "He came in a stable once. That's a kind of garage. Also, notice that Hampton did not need any converts to his religion. He needed no one to support the reality of the voices he heard in his garage. The need to convert others to what we believe can be dangerous, for it can blind us to the truth when it appears, as we saw in the story about the Reverend Sam.

"But look again at the photographs in that Time *article. See the dynamic intensity of Hampton's creations. Perhaps only such a personal religion, the result of a religious experience that is wholly one's own, is truly alive. Only such an experience-fed religion has the power to electrify the imagination and to breathe fire into junk! Who knows, George, maybe the* true *Church is only a holy umbrella linking together a multitude of uniquely personal religions which have arisen from deep prayer, faith and listening hearts. Imagine countless personal religions in harmony with the Way, but with their own sacraments, rituals and feast days! A belief*

133

based on someone else's experience of God may be commendable, but are secondhand religions ever truly dynamic or redemptive? I believe that each person is intended to experience God firsthand and to live out what has been seen and felt."

"Yes," I replied, "Hampton's old brick garage, which smelled of old tires, grease and oil was a listening place for him as this garage has been for me. And if I were to tell my neighbors what I have seen and heard here, they would think I am as insane as James Hampton, who carted all that junk into his garage."

"You have heard a message, George," said Igor, "as have James Hampton and thousands upon thousands of others. They heard it in all sorts of places: garages, bedrooms, factories and fields. Amateur radio operators, who vastly outnumber professional scientists in monitoring messages from outer space, will surely hear communications from other civilizations first. It is the same with those who hear messages from God. You and James Hampton are not theologians: you are, we might say, amateur God-listeners. Saturday after Saturday you have faithfully come here to listen, and your patience and your quiet heart have been rewarded. You have heard more than you have understood. As you are able to translate it into real situations, you will find yourself understanding more and more of what you have heard."

"You have been my guide and mentor," I said. "Will you be around to help me if I get stuck?" The silence that followed my question was as filled with unspoken power as a thunderhead that towers upward in a summer sky.

"Don't worry, my friend," Igor replied, leaning closer. "Once you set foot on the Path, you're never alone. Don't be afraid, I won't desert you when you need me."

134

I sighed in relief and, realizing how late it was, said good night. As I prepare to leave, the image of James Hampton rushing to complete his Sanctuary for the end he knew to be at hand fills my mind with uneasiness. May this apprehension not prevent me from being attentive to my family tonight.

A Homemade Ikon of St. George

St. George, pray for me!

Saturday, July 19th

How good it is to be back in my hermitage again! While I enjoyed the vacation over the holiday with my family, I missed my time here. I wonder if Igor came while I was gone? Surely he knew I wasn't here; my car was not in the garage and the house was locked. Besides, he seems to know everything that happens in my life.

I am eager to begin my quest. Surely I am ready to travel with him. Perhaps we can set a date for our expedition when he comes today.

Noon

Ate a simple meal. No sign yet of my friend. Re-read the Time *article on James Hampton, reflecting on his dying before he had finished his Sanctuary. Or maybe he didn't just die — I mean like other people die. Maybe the Third Heaven of the Nations Millenium General Assembly* did *come to that old brick garage in Washington, D.C. And perhaps as it exploded in cosmic splendor, James Hampton stopped being the sanctuary designer and became an eternal attendant at the throne of God!*

3:00 p.m.

No sign of Igor yet. I'm concerned. I'm spending the day in quiet listening.

4:00 p.m.

Just as I was giving up, he arrived at my door. When I asked him how soon we could leave on our quest, he answered, "Are you sure you're ready? Are you sure you know the cost of such a trip?"

"I'm not sure," I replied. "What kind of cost are you talking about — financial, emotional or physical?"

"George, I'm sure you already have been paying the price for your freedom and new life in many ways," Igor replied. "Nothing in life is free — especially life!"

"True, but it has not been very hard. It does take constant care, but over the weeks and months the effort has become easier. But I'm ready to go beyond where I am now."

"Before you say that and fully mean it," he answered, "let me tell you another story."

Once upon a time, long ago, a great spiritual master gathered all his disciples and followers around him. Lovingly he spoke to them, "My friends, it is time for me to return to my Father. Where I now go, you cannot follow. But do not be sad, for I will come back and take you with me to live forever in paradise."

At this announcement the small band of faithful disciples wept and pleaded with him not to leave. But in spite of their tears and pleas, the Master took them out to a high mountain where he blessed them and tried to comfort them with words of love and encouragement. Then with his arms raised to the sky and his eyes heavenward, he prayed, "Father, I am ready." Slowly the Master began to rise from the earth.

The small band of faithful followers buried their faces in their hands and wept. One of them, however, the close friend and intimate disciple of the Master, cried out, "O Master, don't leave me — I love you!" Suddenly the disciple jumped upward and grasped the Master's ankle!

The Master stalled in midair, listing to one side as his disciple dangled below. As they both hung motionless above the earth, the Master exclaimed, "Let go, my friend, let go. You know that I must ascend to my Father, but you are not ready. You must still be purified. Now . . . let GO!"

But the stubborn adherent did *not* let go as he had been commanded. In fact, he clung to the ankle even more persistently and continued to plead, "O take me with you, dear friend. I cannot live without you!"

The Master looked heavenward and prayed, "Father, what am I to do?"

At that moment a great cloud overshadowed the mountain top, and a voice spoke like a rumble of thunder: "Ascend, my beloved, ascend!" So, with no little effort, the Master began again to ascend with his beloved disciple dangling from his left leg.

Now I need not tell you that the mood on the mountain underwent a radical change while all of this was happening. The mood shifted from deep sorrow to open anger. The close and special relationship (and a very particular friendship it was) between the disciple and the Master had always been a sore point in the small band of disciples . . . and now this! The rest of the followers began shouting to the disciple who dangled from the Master's leg, "Let go, let go. You're holding the Master back! Let go, you fool!" The crowd, composed of the Master's mother and relatives, as well as countless others who had accompanied the disciples and Master up the mountain, all looked on in amazement as the disciples jumped up and down and shook their fists in the air.

Suddenly, the Master's mother ran from the crowd and, with a great leap, grabbed her son's other ankle. Once again the ascension of the

Master came to a halt with a sudden jerk. Looking down, he saw his own mother dangling below. "Mother!" he cried out in frustration. "You, of *all* people, know that I cannot stay. You know that I must return to my heavenly Father. Mother, *please* let go!"

But his mother, like his close friend, only clung tighter to her son's leg and looked up at him with a sweet smile. The Master tried to shake her loose, but that failed. Then, looking heavenward, he cried out in a loud voice, "Father, what am I to do?" A great rumble of thunder shook the mountain top. The crowd on the peak and the three suspended in midair were silent as a voice from the cloud spoke, "Ascend, my beloved, ascend!"

Once again, mustering all his strength, the spiritual Master began ever so slowly to move upward, his friend clinging to his left ankle and his mother hanging to his right. At that moment, as if some invisible signal had been given, all the disciples ran forward and began jumping into the air, grabbing legs and ankles, wrists and arms. And seconds later the rest of the crowd began jumping up to grasp the disciples. Those already airborn reached down to offer hands to those still on the ground.

Then, out of the forest that crowned the mountain top, came bears and foxes, birds and bugs, flowers and bushes, and they too jumped upward and were given a hand. Now what had begun as a beautiful religious experience had suddenly been turned into a circus act! And, as the spiritual Master ascended, a vast pyramid of people, animals and vegetation rose into the sky over the mountain top.

At that moment, the spiritual Master was enlightened! At that very moment he understood his true mission in life for the first time. His purpose on earth was not to be a savior, a son of God or even a saint. His real purpose was to be a giant skyhook!

Once again Igor's done it. With a magician's sleight of hand he had shown me the cost of the next step. Others will want to hang on and rise with me. I suppose there are no private saints, no private quests that the whole human family does not share. Those around us will reach out and take hold as I have risen by holding on to my friend the dragon. "I understand and accept that reality," I responded. "Is there a cost beyond that?"

"It's more difficult to accept than it seems because it requires a great deal of humility. To be the source of others ascent is indeed a position that can inflate the ego. But it can also be very humbling, for it means that people are using you. Many reject being used as an offense to their dignity, but it's all part of the same mystery. Tonight, George, is Saturday night, and that's a special night. To understand what I'm talking about, we should go downtown to the Strip. It's too bad that you have to have dinner with your family. You and I could see the sights and learn a most important lesson from those who belong to what is called the world's oldest profession."

"What kind of man do you take me to be?" I asked, a bit angry at Igor's suggestion. "I'm happily married, and I have no need for anything that such a woman could offer me!"

"Really!" Igor replied with a smile. "Allow me to enlighten you. Before you get too indignant, I'll tell you a story — just as the man it happened to told it to me. You can never tell what you might learn on the street . . . ."

140

I'll never forget her or that night. She was standing on the corner of 12th and Vine, wearing a red dress whose hem was high above her knees. With her lips painted to match her dress, she smiled at each passer-by. Her eyes, filled with invitation, called out to one and all. Now keep in mind that I'm not the sort of man who takes up with *that* kind of woman, but those eyes . . . and those lips, slightly curved in a smile that held the promise of delights beyond imagination.

She suggested that we go to her apartment around the corner, and I agreed, being a stranger in town. It was small — not more than two rooms. I quickly sank into a faded easy chair and began talking about the weather, politics and anything I could think of to cover my embarrassment. I knew she worked by the hour, and yet she just sat there patiently listening to me. There was no pushiness about her.

As I said, I was embarrassed. I just don't do that sort of thing. The palms of my hands were all sweaty. I talked nervously about myself, my job, my wife and family. I used some carefully chosen words so she would know that I was no ordinary guy off the street. Oh no, I had an education — I was *somebody*. She didn't pretend to be anything but herself. And when I bragged about my money and social standing, she showed no signs of jealousy or envy. She didn't seem to care about any of that.

She kept wanting to know if she could get me anything: more ice for my drink . . . was the chair comfortable? My needs seemed to be all she could think of. But that's her profession, right? I wondered if she had been trained by one of those Japanese Geisha girls you read about. She was so polite and seemed to need nothing herself.

But I was still uncomfortable, so I fished

around for something else to talk about. I asked her about her life — if she had always been on the street. She told me that she began only after the man she had married had dumped her with no money and no place to stay. She loved him, but she said he was "sort of mixed up, crazy in the head." He would lock her in the closet whenever he left, and he beat her up a lot. One day he just threw her out, after beating her terribly. There was not a trace of resentment in her voice. She told her story as if it had happened a thousand years ago to another person. When people tell you their troubles, they sound as if they have been sitting on them, brooding over them like mother hens. But her voice was quiet and calm.

I asked if she had ever heard from the guy again. Not directly, she told me. But she heard he'd gotten mixed up with some gang of hoods. They double-crossed him, and he was sent to the pen on a phoney conviction. As she talked, her voice was edged in sadness. That confused me, and I asked, "Didn't he get what was coming to him? That's exactly what he deserved."

But she said, "No, that's not the way life *should* be."

As the night slowly turned into dawn, the neon lights outside her window flashed off. The sun was about to rise over the air conditioning units on top of the buildings across the street. I had grown fond of this hooker. She was full of hope for the world, even though she had been exploited at every turn. She had a trust that is common in little children but not in adults. Everything was going to turn out for the best, even if all that had happened so far seemed to prove it wasn't true.

As the sun crested the buildings, I slowly got up from the faded easy chair where I had sat all night. I took out my billfold to offer her some money. She shook her head and smiled, saying that she didn't charge anything.

I stopped at the door, realizing how rude I had been. "Excuse me. I never even asked your name."

She looked at me with great fondness. Then with a self-contained little smile, she replied, "The name, my dear, is LOVE. What's yours?"

We sat in silence a few moments after he had finished. Then Igor asked me to read aloud from St. Paul's letter to the Corinthians:

Love is patient; love is kind. Love is not jealous, it does not put on airs, it is not snobbish. Love is never rude, it is not self-seeking, it is not prone to anger; nor does love brood over injuries. Love does not rejoice over what is wrong but rejoices in the truth. There is no limit to love's forbearance, to its trust, its hope, its power to endure. (1 Cor 13: 4-7)

"No one enjoys being used, George. But in a sense, being used is what it's all about. Anyone who wants to see the Holy Grail must be willing to be used by others — must become a prostitute. But not an ordinary hooker. Many people have been imprisoned by the exploitation of others. But the hooker in the story poured out her love with no strings attached, transforming the experience of being used into an act of genuine service. She was patient beyond reason, never putting on airs or being proud of her humility. Love is never self-seeking, never broods over past injuries. It knows no limits, and that means there is no point where it stops and says, 'That's it, no more!' Are you sure you're ready for the journey to the Land of No Limits?"

As I write this, I know that I didn't say what I felt.

"Of course I'm ready!" is what I said. But deep within my heart, my spirit whispered, "I hope I can love like that, but I'm afraid I'll give up in pain and exhaustion if there are no limits to my love. I thought God is the only one who can love without limits."

Igor sat there, radiant and magnificent, looking deeply into my eyes. I had the feeling what he heard was not my words but the small voice of my spirit deep inside. His wounds glowed in the late afternoon twilight with a brilliance that I had not seen since that first night when we had traveled together in the darkness of the forest. I couldn't help wondering if they were wounds caused by loving without conditions or limits.

"All right, comrade," Igor said, rising to his feet, "then all is ready for the quest of the Holy Grail. I shall return in two weeks time. Put your life in order: make out your will, conclude any unresolved personal matters and say good-bye to those you love. But think about it carefully. If you decide that this is not the time, simply leave a large, white bed sheet on the side of the garage as a signal. If I see the sign, I promise I'll return in another two weeks to visit you." Then, without even saying "good-bye" or "see you later," he simply disappeared into thin air.

As I write this, the twilight has turned to dusk, and I hesitate to go to the house. My wife will know that something has happened. How I hate to tell her that this time it is real, that this time I am really going.

Saturday, July 26th

Spent the entire day in silence. Simply sat and listened. All I heard was the wind in the cottonwood trees.

"WHEN ALL THE TIES
THAT BIND THE HEART
ARE LOOSENED,
WHAT REMAINS THEN?"

TAT TWAM ASI...
YOU ARE THAT!"

Katha Upanishads

Saturday, August 2nd

It is five and one-half months since I began coming here to the garage to spend time alone. This morning as I walked from the house to the garage, it seemed twice as far as from here to the sun. With each step, I wanted to turn back and run into the house. I could see my wife as she wept in the kitchen. In these few months we have grown to love each other even more than when we were young lovers. How strange it is that the more you love God the more you love others. She begged me not to leave on the quest. Secretly, I had hoped that she could talk me out of it. But in my heart I knew that it wasn't possible. I'm consumed with this passion. I have to find the Holy Grail. In a way it doesn't make any sense. I don't even know for sure if the Holy Grail ever existed. Maybe it's just a symbol. Anyway, I've packed just a few things in a backpack — what can you take on a quest but a pure heart? This time I'm sure not taking that damn sword.

It's mid-morning as I write this. I've tried to sit in silence, but my heart and head are too full of thoughts. They thunder inside me, and it's impossible to be quiet — but I'm trying. Maybe that's all anyone can ever do. I hope we are measured by how much we try rather than how quiet it actually is inside us.

There is so much that I want to say to whoever reads this journal. This will be my last entry. I won't take it with me on the quest.

It's noon and there's still no sign of my friend. Martha has looked out the kitchen door every hour. I wave to her and she retreats into the shadows. Perhaps she is praying that Igor won't come. I'll miss being with her this Saturday night. Those nights, *after a full day alone, have been so intimate and powerful. I will miss her and them.*

Igor finally arrived around mid-afternoon. His eagerness lifted my somber spirits, and I quickly gathered a few things from my makeshift desk and stuck them into my backpack.

"What's that?" asked Igor.

"My backpack. Only one change of clothing, a few toilet articles, my passport and some bare essentials for our journey," I answered, trying to hide my pride in being able to travel so simply.

"George," Igor said, speaking with surprise, "when you leave on a quest, you must travel with simplicity. We don't have room for all that luggage!"

His word "luggage" pierced my pride: he made it sound as if I had two steamer trunks and five suitcases. "It's only the barest of necessities," I said defensively. "It took me days to cut it down to just what would fit in this backpack."

"Remember the story about the young man who came to Jesus seeking eternal life?" Igor asked me with that tone of voice when he was about to tell a story. "Remember how Jesus told the young man that if he wanted to be his follower, he must go and sell all that he possessed. Well, George, the same is true for you! But allow me the pleasure of a story to further illustrate this.

He was a stranger in a strange city, with a free night and nothing to do. As he strolled along the main street, he absorbed, with casual interest, the sights and sounds of this unknown city. He turned a corner on Main Street and found the street that every city owns but would like to disown. It was a street filled with bars, nightclubs, striptease joints, porno shops and adult bookstores. A brief shower had transformed the black asphalt street

148

into a glistening mirror which caught the neon lights in brilliant green, blue and red rippling reflections.

Here and there between the bars and glittering night spots were dark, narrow doorways. Prostitutes, male and female, stood waiting — half-hidden from the rain-washed night. As the stranger walked past the bars, their neon lights and loud, jarring music mingled to form a tantalizing promise of pleasure, companionship and entertainment. As he passed each door, he looked in but did not enter. On his left the street was filled with slowly cruising cars — the lonely figures inside riding the thin edge of temptation.

In the middle of the block, between an adult bookstore and a country-western bar, was a small nightclub whose neon light flashed out, THE HIMALAYAN HOT SPOT . . . EXOTIC ENTERTAINMENT AND DRINKS FROM THE ORIENT. He stopped to look at the gaudy poster next to the entrance, outlined in blinking white lights. It read, COME IN AND SEE DOLLY LAMA, THE TIBETAN SPRIPTEASER. From inside the club he could hear the sounds of Tibetan drums, whose rhythm drew him toward the door with a strange magnetic charm.

The stranger found himself opening the door of the Himalayan Hot Spot and stepping inside. His eyes took a moment to focus in the dimly lit interior, a misty blur of candles and red and yellow spotlights. An oriental waiter, wearing the robes of a Tibetan Buddhist monk, silently ushered him to a small round table with a single chair. The table, illuminated by a single flickering candle, was on the far edge of a circle of pale yellow light which outlined the dance floor. The waiter took his order for a drink, bowed and silently slipped away. As the stranger's eyes became accustomed to the dim light, he observed that the walls of the club were hung with deep red Tibetan rugs covered with intricate designs; interspersed with the rugs were multi-colored mandalas outlined with gold. The waiters, all dressed as monks, moved among the tables set back in the darkness. A cloud of cigarette smoke and incense hung in the room. At the bar was the usual population of sailors, a few hookers, and solitary men, staring dully into the mirror behind the bar. The room was pulsating with Tibetan music, coming from a small combo of drums, chimes and long mountain horns.

Suddenly, without warning, a large brass gong sounded! The music and all conversation stopped, and the air became charged with anticipation. Once again the giant brass gong rang, and the drums, chimes and horns began to play a wild folk song, as a slim Oriental woman danced through the glass beaded curtains at the far end of the club. As she whirled exotically around the yellow circle of light in the center of the club, the tiny brass castinets on her fingers clicked in perfect time to the music. "This must be Dolly Lama herself!" thought the stranger. "What a beautiful woman — what a superb dancer!"

Dolly Lama was dressed in layers of purple and orange silken scarves that whirled about her like prayer flags flapping in the winds of Nepal. As she danced past the stranger, she looked directly at him, her eyes dark and searching. With each turn around the dance floor she came closer and closer to his table until, slowly and seductively, she circled him alone.

The drums pounded hypnotically in an ever-increasing tempo as she wound her way around him with serpentine gestures. When he felt her hands on him, he sat bolt upright in his chair,

150

breathing rapidly. Her hands moved with silky smoothness upon his body. Suddenly the music and the dancer stopped! Dolly Lama stood in front of him, holding his billfold in her hand. "Who are you?" she asked.

Absolute silence froze the nightclub. The stranger cleared his throat in an effort to regain his composure and said, "It's all there on my I.D. cards in that billfold you're holding." He thought to himself, "If I get out of this place without losing anything more than my money, I'll be lucky! What a stupid thing it was to come in here in the first place!"

The Tibetan stripteaser slowly removed his professional card, which identified his position in his company, from the billfold's accordian folder. As she handed it to him, he was amazed to see that the card was completely blank! Smiling, Dolly Lama said, "This card tells me nothing. Who are you?"

The stranger looked at his billfold in dismay and said, "Examine my other cards: my driver's license, passport, birth certificate, my insurance and credit cards." As Dolly produced each card, the printing on it disappeared! His profession, his name, his sexual identity, age, marital status, the signs of his success — his country club member-ship and credit cards — were all blank! Now the Tibetan drums rumbled like thunder as Dolly Lama handed back his billfold. Not a single dollar bill was missing — but where was his identity? The paradox was overwhelming! The famous Tibetan stripteaser had not removed a garment, not a single silken scarf! It was *he* who had been stripped!

He felt totally hollow, valueless, impotent — frightened, alone and confused. As the drums rumbled softly, the flutes and horns rose in

151

volume. Their music was like the snow, like white wind howling through steep icy canyons, "WHO ARE YOU, WHO ARE YOU, WHO ARE YOU???"

Dolly Lama leaned close, her face next to his, the exotic perfume of armfuls of Himalayan wildflowers flooding his nostrils. Then she whispered a single short sentence into his ear. The great temple gong rang out and the drums and horns again began their mysterious music. Dolly sprang to her feet, whirled like a child's top around the pale circle of light and disappeared through the beaded curtain.

The stranger, who now was *truly* a stranger even to himself, bolted from his chair and rushed for the exit. As he ran wildly into the flashing neon-lit night, he cried aloud, "That's madness . . . insanity! What she whispered is impossible! It's heresy . . . heresy!"

When Igor had finished and allowed me some time to think about his story, I spoke. "I can understand how the stranger felt in being totally stripped of his identity; I too feel dazed at the thought."

"It's a paralyzing prospect," Igor said. "But think back to the very first story I told you about the escape from prison."

"I thought I was ready to go through the escape tunnel," I said. "I understand, Igor, that escaping and finding freedom is at the heart of the quest for the Holy Grail. But must I take nothing with me, not even my own name?"

He did not answer at once. He watched a butterfly that was ascending and descending on a leaf outside the hermitage window. After a long silence he spoke, "My friend, as Jesus looked with love upon the young man who wanted to find Life, I look at you. How difficult it is for us to have the courage to use the escape tunnel. And how afraid society is that we will use it and begin a great exodus! I believe that Jesus was saying to the young man, 'You seem to want something more than a sense of righteousness and security: you want LIFE. If you do, then realize that the escape tunnel is so narrow, cramped and tiny that you can get through it only if you are naked! You must be stripped of more than possessions. You must be naked of what possessions represent: title, name, reputation, role, personality — every trace of your false self. Only the truest self that is wedded to the divine spark can remain.'"

We both sat in silence as I fearfully wondered if I could leave on the quest completely naked. Would that mean that I must even be physically naked? To be clothed is itself a form of protection and status. Does Igor mean that I am worthy to start only when I am completely dispossessed? I closed my eyes, seeking answers from my own heart. When I opened them, I was alone. Igor, with great sensitivity, had

"Anyone who does not take up his/her cross and follow me cannot be my disciple."

Jesus
The gospel of Luke

slipped away silently as I pondered this last require-
ment. I sat in the darkness of my hermitage and
stared at the moon which had risen full and yellow.
I saw it in all its beauty, but I was really looking
beyond the moon and into myself. Back in March I
had not realized that my desire to set out on a quest
would lead to all this. I am beginning to understand
that it is a long, long process — and a painful one.
Now I understand, with my heart, the words of Jesus
when he said that those who wished to follow him
must take up their crosses and die to themselves. I
realize that dying is at the heart of the very call to
follow Jesus or to seek out the Holy Grail, and that
hearing one's real name pronounced also means
bearing the cost. I understand that the way is not
easy, but I cannot turn back. These past months have
been the most exciting of my life, and I am beginning
to see that it will be this challenging for the rest of
my life. Have patience, Lord, as I come with halting
steps in search of the Holy Grail.

It's past 9 p.m. as this disappointed knight of the
Holy Grail picks up his backpack and prepares to
return to the house. Martha will be delighted, and
I long to be in her understanding arms.

Saturday, August 16th

I wasn't home last Saturday. Martha's mother died, and all our family went to the funeral. I didn't leave a note on my hermitage door; somehow Igor knows everything without my having to tell him.

The funeral was a sobering event, and I realized why we try so hard to hide from the reality of death. Sitting there as the choir sang and all the rituals took place, I couldn't help thinking about my last conversation with Igor. Is this the only way out, I wonder? Is death the only escape from pain and suffering, from the daily struggle to find a little happiness in the prison of existence? Is this the only way to be totally without identity? And is the Quest itself an exercise in make-believe, only something to give me a sense of hope and promise? Is the Quest real? Is Igor real?

Today I am not at all geared up to leave with Igor. I feel that his wordless departure two weeks ago is a sign that I needed more time. He was right. In my visions of those who set out looking for the Holy Grail, no one was naked. They were dressed in glistening silver armor, and they looked like heroes. Who ever saw a naked hero?

I promised Martha that I would not leave today — maybe next week or the one after, but not today. She seemed relieved and asked me to tell her more about this Holy Grail that I'm going off to look for.

I told her that, according to the legend, the Holy Grail is the cup that Jesus used at the Last Supper. I explained that Joseph of Arimathea is said to have used the Grail to catch some of Jesus' blood as it fell from the cross. Then he carried the cup to England and placed it in a church which he built himself. Medieval legends throughout Europe describe how, through the years, this source of holy energy was moved from place to place. It was said to be guarded by angels who prevented anyone who wasn't pure from finding it. Countless knights have gone on adventures to look for it but have failed to bring it back. Now it has become a symbol of Life, Peace and Happiness. It is another word for Heaven, the Ultimate State of Consciousness, the Bosom of Abraham, Enlightenment, Life Everlasting, Cosmic Mindfulness, Satori, Fana, Samadhi, the Wu of Taoism, the Mystic Rose, the Star of David, the Thousand Petalled Lotus, the Clear Mirror and more.

But Martha only shook her head and smiled. "Why," she asked me, "would you want to seek any of those things?"

Her question was a logical one, but I fear I did not give her a logical answer. I told her that I didn't set out to seek anything, neither the Holy Grail nor the Thousand Petalled Lotus, but whatever it was came seeking me!

About noon, Martha came to the back door of the house and called me. She said that I had a phone call from Igor and that he said it was most urgent. I took the call on the extension in our bedroom.

"Is that you, George?" I recognized the dragon's voice.

"Yes, Igor, it's me, but what . . . ?"

"I hate to bother you while you're in solitude, but I want to tell you that I just won't be able to come today. Something important has happened, George, and someone in my position isn't always free. I just didn't want you to worry or draw the wrong conclusions."

Behind his voice I could hear the sounds of traffic. Was he calling from a pay phone? "That's alright, Igor," I replied. "I understand. Will you be coming next Saturday?"

"Yes, and be ready if you still want to leave. Do

you have any questions?"

The thoughts raced madly through my mind — was I ready? I wasn't sure. I had too many questions about our last visit. "I know you're in a hurry, Igor," I said, "but I don't know just what you meant when you said I had to leave on the quest naked. Did you mean that literally?"

"To find what you seek, George," answered Igor, "you must leave behind not only your possessions but everything you hold dear. You must be stripped of all that you have been told gives you life, all that you believe and have been told is valuable and necessary. Only then will you find the one thing you seek."

"Let me pray about that," I answered, using an expression that was not normally part of my speech. "By next Saturday I think I will be ready to go with you in search of the Holy Grail, taking absolutely nothing with me."

"Good, I am eager to begin the journey," came the reply from the other end of the line. "I look forward to seeing you. Oh, by the way, George, next Saturday when you come to your hermitage, don't forget to bring the garbage!"

"The garbage?" I asked in complete bewilderment.

"Yes, that's right. See you next week. Bye, George." And the phone went dead before I could ask any more questions.

I'm getting ready to close up my hermitage at the end of this most unusual day. As I do, the question "Am I ready?" still haunts me.

Saturday, August 23rd

It's mid-morning as I enter this account in my journal. I told Martha and the children good-bye again this morning. As I did I tried to invest that usually empty expression with as much "good" as I could. I tried to fill each letter of those words with love, gratitude and blessing. Martha had tears in her eyes, fearful that this was indeed to be the day. The children think my continuous "final" departures are some sort of game. They playfully told me good-bye, and the oldest said, "See you at supper, Daddy." When I filled the black plastic bag with all the garbage in the house, Martha just shook her head. I didn't even attempt to explain what I was doing — I don't even know myself! What love that woman has, to believe in me when everything I do or say sounds insane.

The day grows hot, and my hermitage smells like the inside of an old garbage can. I have all the windows open, and it's still potent. Igor will need a lot of magic to transform these old coffee grounds, meat scraps, spoiled fruit and trash into something worthwhile. I'm tempted to leave the bag outside, but Igor might think I'm uncomfortable with it as traveling equipment. Who knows — perhaps I will have to take it with me as is, so I'd best get used to the smell of it.

Noon

No sign of Igor yet. With the August sun heating up the garbage bag, I'm not hungry.

Mid-afternoon

I had fallen asleep when a gentle knock at my door-

160

post awoke me. There was Igor, smiling and holding a claw to his great nose. "I see you didn't forget the garbage, George," Igor said as he came inside. Before I could say a word, he continued, "I know this sounds like a most unusual requirement for a mythical journey. But here is a story that may help explain it.

Once there was a garbage man who worked in the little Midwestern town of Pleasant Hill. He drove a battered, blue Ford pickup truck with makeshift sideboards that rose twelve feet or more above the truck bed. He worked alone except for his ever-present companion, Spot, a white and brown dog with a ring around its eye. Spot was the friendliest dog in town and barked only at the other dogs who set up a racket whenever the garbage man appeared.

He was a familiar town character, and the only name people called him was "the Garbage Man." The ladies who sat on their porches, wearing white linen dresses, said he was of "mixed blood." He wasn't black and he wasn't brown. He seldom spoke or was spoken to by those whose garbage and trash he hauled away. He was dirty and he smelled; it was, shall we say, a by-product of his profession. The only unique thing about the Garbage Man was the tattoo on the back of his weathered right hand — a red heart inscribed with the words, "I LOVE YOU."

The Garbage Man drove daily up and down the alleys of the town, with Spot sitting next to him in the cab of the old pickup. He took an unusual interest in his work — not only did he empty the stinking and overflowing garbage cans that stood at the back gates and garages of homes, but he also picked up trash that people had dumped along the roadsides and in dry creek beds.

161

The Garbage Man had made the town of Pleasant Hill not only pleasant but beautiful. While this was reason to admire his unique profession, the townsfolk thought he was not as admirable as he was "simple." Apparently he could not read or write, for he never sent a monthly bill for his work. He would graciously accept any payment from a customer, but some didn't think to pay him for months at a time. Others simply thought the removal of trash was one of the services provided by City Hall. And this voluntary pickup of trash along the roadway? Well, it was just another sign that he wasn't too bright.

The Garbage Man and Spot lived alone, somewhere north of town. The gossip was that he was divorced or that his wife had left him. Small wonder — who would want to be married to a garbage collector? People did see him with a few friends at the end of the day before he headed out of town with his truckload of garbage. They were, well, the white trash of town — men and women that hung out around the bar and pool hall down by the railroad tracks.

The Garbage Man was a mystery that aroused little curiosity, except from little children. As he drove down the alley with Spot's head hanging out the side window, the children would ask their mothers, "Where does that man take the garbage?" And their mothers, shooing their children out of the kitchen, would answer, "To the dump, dear. Now run outside and play." And that was the extent of the curiosity about the man of "mixed blood" with the heart tattooed on his right hand.

The Garbage Man was reliable — most of the time. Sometimes he would fail to appear for several days. It was rumored that he went on drinking binges. But who wouldn't be tempted to get drunk, handling stinking garbage all day long? One day he failed to appear; that day grew into two, then four, then seven. The garbage cans of Pleasant Hill overflowed as trash, litter and junk spilled over into the alleys. The stink was terrible, and the complaints rose like high tide under a full moon.

The part-time mayor — and full-time owner of the hardware store — and the town's police chief decided that they should go and see what had happened. They headed north out of town to find the Garbage Man. No one knew for sure where he lived, since no one had visited his small farm. The road ran through a timber of tall cottonwoods, and soon they saw a battered mailbox, half-falling off its post. Painted in crude, childlike letters on its side was "GARBAGE PICKUP." They turned off the county road on to a deeply rutted dirt track that led back into the timber. As they drove along, they could see pieces of paper and tin cans scattered along the side of the road.

The road grew narrower and more rutted as they traveled back into the hills. Cresting a hilltop, the mayor slammed on the brakes of his car. He and the police chief gasped in disbelief! Before them was a little valley with a tumble-down, un-painted shack and a rickety, swaybacked barn in the center. But what held them in wordless shock was that the entire valley was filled with garbage — mountains of trash, cans and bottles, rusted bodies of old cars and broken-down furniture! The stench was breathtaking.

As they drove down into the valley, between the towering mounds of garbage, the mayor kept repeating, "My God, my God — he took all the garbage home with him!" As their car came out of the end of the tunnel of trash, they saw Spot in front of the run-down house, sitting beside a giant

163

pile of garbage. They got out of the car, but Spot didn't move or bark. She just sat and looked at them. When the two men came close, they saw it. Next to her paw, sticking out of a landslide of garbage, was a hand tattooed with a red heart and the words, "I LOVE YOU."

"ONLY THE ONE WHO TAKES
UPON ONESELF THE
EVILS OF THE WORLD
MAY BE ITS SAVIOR."

Tao Te Ching

We sat in silence for a long time. Then Igor opened my garbage bag and said, "You've only brought your garbage, George! It stinks to high heaven, but it's only a small symbol of the real garbage that you must be willing to carry — not just your garbage but the garbage of everyone who lives in your town . . . and the world! Are you willing to own all that terrible mess? Only if you are, will you be able to bear the title 'St.' with honesty. For until now you would not have been able to understand that those initials stand not only for Sent *or* Saint *but also for the most mysterious of all titles,* Servant.*"*

I sat in a dense fog of confusion. It's hard enough to own my own hate and anger, prejudices and petty discriminations, but to be expected to own the sinfulness of others doesn't seem fair. Why should I have to take on the dirt of those who sexually abuse children, who lie, cheat and murder, who keep the poor chained to poverty? But I also felt the tidal pull of the Mystery, the Holy Grail, calling me to move on.

Igor spoke quietly, "You are a free man, just as you were at the beginning of our friendship. The choice is yours. You see, George the Sent, Saint and Servant, only when you are able to see that you are more than an isolated individual, that you are a part of everyone, will you be able to see the Holy Grail. Remember that even Perceval, the brave and pure knight in the Grail legend, wandered for years lost on the quest. The image of the Grail faded in and out until he found the answer to the great question, 'Whom does the Grail serve?' Until you have grown to that awareness, the adventure is doomed from the beginning. You have the grace to reach that final consciousness; all you need now is the desire to live it out."

We both sat quietly. He respected my hesitation and appreciated that this last requirement was contrary to everything I had learned. After awhile, he touched my hand fondly. "Think about it, George — but not just with your rational mind. You must open your Kopavi!"

I remembered reading in the Book of the Hopi that there were several vibratory centers along the axis of the body which echoed the primal sounds of life in the universe. The first of these lay at the top of the head and was called the Kopavi. It was the soft spot, the "open door" through which the creator first communicated and breathed life into human beings. When the Hopi were in difficulty, they would stop, open the doors at the top of their heads and let themselves be guided. When they did this, the creator led them to the "place of emergence."

"If you can open this door and make the decision, we will begin the search for the Holy Grail. Seven days from now is August the 30th. It's the Saturday before Labor Day. Spend that weekend with your family. If you decide to go with me, be ready on Monday morning, September 8th, at sunrise. That's always been a special day for me. In Medieval Europe it was celebrated with feasting and parades as the birthday of Mary, the Virgin Mother of God. Traditionally it was the day for swallows to leave Austria for Italy. It was the day herds of cattle decorated with autumn flowers were driven down from the meadows of the Alps. September the 8th is a day for departures, and it will hold good luck and magic for us. But remember, if you choose not to go, I will understand.

Igor smiled one of his great dragon smiles and disappeared. Sitting here with my garbage, I feel sad, frightened and confused. Like the young man who was invited to follow Jesus, I have many cherished possessions. Can I bear to leave them behind and carry the garbage instead? I wonder if I'm that strong
. . . .

166

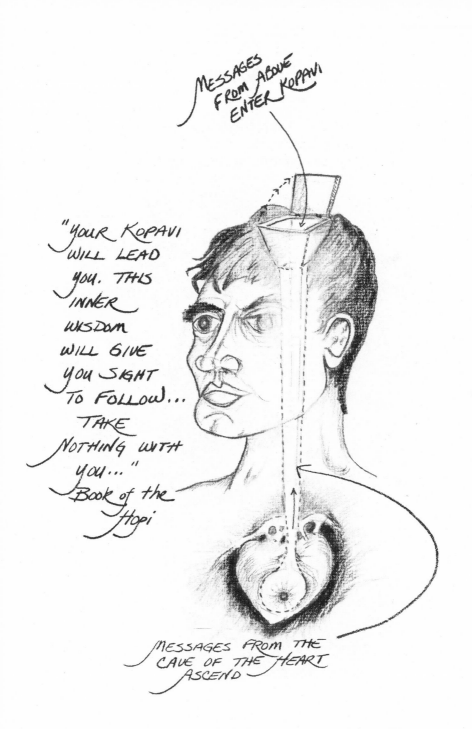

Saturday, August 30th

Wanted to spend this early morning in solitude, sorting things out, so that I can enjoy the rest of the Labor Day weekend with my family.

Saturday, September 6th

Like last Saturday, I'm spending some time in quiet solitude, trying to sit as simply as possible with all my questions about leaving on the quest. I feel I need to create enough space inside for the decision to make itself, enough space to hear the quiet voice of guidance.

I just briefly want to record something that happened last night. In one clear moment I caught a glimpse of what being a real servant means. Most of us get buried by the weight of the garbage of others before we become radiant — like Igor's wounds — through our service. But in that one moment I really saw the great love of Jesus which bears the sins and troubles of everyone. I could feel the great measure of love necessary to understand true servanthood. I had a vision of Martha as old and ill, and in that moment I understood the glorious gift it can be to care for a loved one made feeble by age. I was held by such a great love that I was not weighed down by the burden of that care. It was a wonderful moment, and I still feel its effects, but I'm not sure it makes my decision to leave with Igor on our quest any easier.

In the pre-dawn darkness I make this last entry in my journal. I have chosen to go with Igor on the quest for the Holy Grail. I didn't say good-bye to my children but kissed them as they slept, with all my heart's love. I traced the sign of the cross above them, and I asked God to bless them. I pray that I may see them again someday. Last night's dinner was so rich, so full of love, but it was also seasoned with deep sadness. All through the meal Martha looked at me as if she were trying to memorize me. The food, laughter and love filled us in every way; and Martha — she was the most beautiful woman in the world. I realized during the meal that I had never seen her before; I had only looked at her. It's strange what makes up a real feast. The ingredients may only be a sip of wine and a small morsel of bread, but if it's flooded with love, it is truly a heavenly banquet.

Whatever happens to me on this quest, wherever I go, the memory of our last night together will always be as vivid and real as it is now. Why am I so drunk with gratitude this morning? What has kept me from beginning every day like this?

I have left all my belongings in the house. Everything precious to me is asleep in the house that used to be mine. I walked across the back yard a few minutes ago and felt the warm wind of these last days of summer on my naked body. I come here as stripped of everything as possible. Will I be worthy, even after all this, to find the Holy Grail? Am I pure enough, as the legend said, to reach it if I carry the filth and slime of the sins of the world? Perhaps that is the ultimate paradox: only when we own that garbage do we truly earn the purity to see God.

The sky is turning turquoise as dawn begins. Here

*and there a bird joins in the overture. As the sound
and color increase, I feel a sense of expectant joy.
On this feast day of the woman who gave birth to the
Son of God, I feel that I am being reborn. Naked as
I came from my own mother's womb, I am now
somehow being born again, as Jesus spoke of being
reborn. I am newly alive — and free!*

*The first rays of the sun shoot through the trees
like a clash of golden cymbals. The glory of it all
pierces my heart as birds, sky, clouds and trees sing
the song of a new day.*

*And then above them all, a rusty but enthusiastic
voice begins to sing:*

> *It's a long way to Tipperary,*
> *It's a long way to go.*
> *It's a long way to Tipperary,*
> *To the sweetest girl I know.*
> *Good-bye Piccadilly, farewell Leicester Square.*
> *It's a long, long way to Tipperary,*
> *But my heart's right there.*

*Over the treetops, with all the grace of a circus
acrobat, with all the beauty of an angel on the wing,
Igor came gliding down to meet me.*

*"Sent, Servant and Saint George," he greeted me,
his great dragon eyes aflame with affection. "I can
see with only half a glance that you're ready to leave.
I'm so proud of you and so happy that you've made
that difficult choice. The air currents are perfect, and
the flying conditions are excellent. What a beautiful
day it is!"*

*I was busy writing these last words and events in
my journal as Igor filled his lungs with the early
morning fresh air. "How do you plan on ending that
journal?" Igor asked.*

*"I'm not sure," I answered. "I've never thought
about that final detail."*

171

"The best stories are the ones without an end," said Igor. "That allows for the possibility of several different endings — or no ending at all!"

"Perhaps I should leave a note for Martha," I said sheepishly, aware that my thought was an indication that I had not left everything behind.

"Perhaps," answered Igor, "if you think you can put into words what words cannot say."

Igor was right. I realized that I had said all that could be said last night when we were together. This was the final stripping. I was free, but I had my wounds. That is always the price. "I'm ready," I said. " 'It's a long way to Tipperary,' so let's be off."

"The Holy Grail," Igor said, "like all precious treasures, is found by those who seek it with all their hearts. 'Seek and you shall find,' as it is said. You, George, have sought it passionately, and the passionate devotion of the seeker is the major work of the Quest." Looking around the hermitage, Igor picked up the mystic mirror he had given me months ago. "You don't want to forget this," he said, handing it to me. "You may be naked as a newborn, but you'll need this."

I took the hermitage mirror in my hand, remembering my fears when I first began to see my own darkness, the dark side hidden by my blindness. As I looked into it now, I saw the garbage — the sin, the weakness, the failings that were once unbearable. I could look into the mirror and say truthfully, "I love you." And this morning I could see that I also bore the darkness and weakness of vast multitudes, of those past and those to come. And as I looked at all that darkness, I could say with complete conviction, "I love you."

Igor smiled as he watched and said, "Turn it over, George, and look in the other side."

Slowly I turned the mirror. There on the other side was the brilliance of ten thousand sunrises —

172

the image blinded me with its intense beauty. And out of the center of the explosion of sunbursts, a golden chalice appeared — the Holy Grail!

My whole being was saturated with light, and my heart throbbed like thunder as I felt my body expanding beyond the furthest reaches of the cosmos.

"Yes, George," said a voice that came from everywhere. " 'Thou art that.' You, George, are the Holy Grail!"

Editorial Note:

That was the last page in the journal of St. George. Perhaps, as Igor said, "The best stories are the ones without an end." Perhaps it is up to each of us to finish this story of the quest for the Holy Grail.

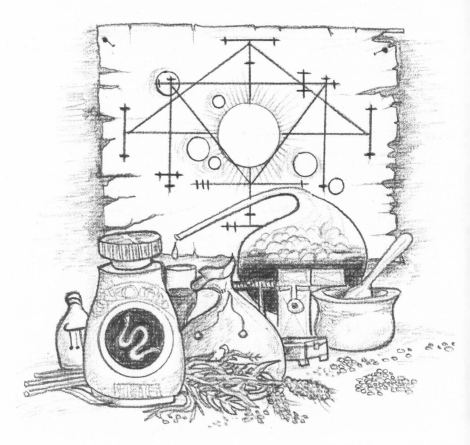

THE MAGIC OF BOOKS

Once upon a time, very long ago, the words of books were truly magical. Only a select few knew the cryptic art of writing or reading the books that contained those words. Those who knew the art belonged to a special and sacred priesthood. Today books are printed by machines, but there is still much magic within. And within this book is the magic of:

THE MAGIC OF WORDS . . .

I am grateful to the editors of this book, who, with great care and no little magic, slowly examined each word as if it were some ancient rune. Their gifts of insight saw to it that each word possesses the maximum magic to open the windows of your mind:

Thomas Skorupa, who was a dedicated alchemist to the birth of this book

and

Ruth Slickman, whose personal love of words and books made her a mage-midwife of the book

and

Jennifer Sullivan, Joanne Meyer, Stephen Daney, Mary Beth Niemann, Sheila Morrow and Thomas Jacobs, whose careful proofreading provided the final charmed touch to the text.

THE MAGIC OF MAKING A BOOK . . .

The supervision of a manuscript's construction and its printing was once the work of temple priests and magi. The following, to whom I am most grateful, performed this intricate office:

Thomas Turkle, president of Forest of Peace Books, Inc., who, as producer and overseer, skillfully integrated its publication

and

David DeRusseau, who added to the book's enchantment by his contribution as the art-design consultant

and

Steve Hall, printer, who directed the mechanical magic of printing and offered valuable suggestions

and

Cliff Hall, printer, who, in his desire for excellence in his ancient craft, watched over the production of the book

and

all their magical assistants at Hall Directory, Inc. in Topeka, Kansas.

THE MAGIC OF FRIENDS . . .

Any work of creativity is a marriage of madness and magic that includes pinches of potent sorcery from friends who sometimes are totally unaware that their enchantment has rubbed off on the author. My gratitude to these and all my friends for their encouragement and gifts of thaumaturgy:

Gerry Hanus
George Steger
Mary Vincentia Maronick
Rupert Pate
George Bellairs
Rita Klarer
Tom Melchior

178

THE AUTHOR'S MAGIC . . .

Edward Hays describes himself as walking the razor's edge between madness and magic. Born in Lincoln, Nebraska, he describes his childhood as being surrounded by silent applause from his parents, his brothers Joe and Tom and his sister Jane.

With that enchanted childhood as a bulletproof vest, he entered adult life—but never totally abandoned the wonder-world of stories and imagination. His professional education was shaped in a magic monastery, Conception Abbey in Missouri, whose Benedictine monks opened his eyes to the location of hidden treasures along the road of life.

He became a Catholic priest and wandered here and there in the mystic land of Kansas, as well as in India and the Orient, seeking, like St. George, the Holy Grail.

Presently he is a rocking chair pilgrim and lives in a community of men and women—east of the moon and west of the sea—who watch daily and attempt to call forth the Sunrise of the Age-that-is-coming.

THE MAGIC OF A GIFT BOOK . . .

If you are fortunate enough to have received this book or any book as a gift, then you know the unique enchantment of a book given as an expression of love. Its presence, long after it has been read, recalls the giver and the giver's love for you. Those books that help us to change our course in life, to see light in the darkness or that call us to greatness are truly gifts from the gods. May the magic of this book, then, be like a time-release capsule that slowly releases its potency—healing and challenging. And by its simple presence may it be a continuously flowing fountain of affection.

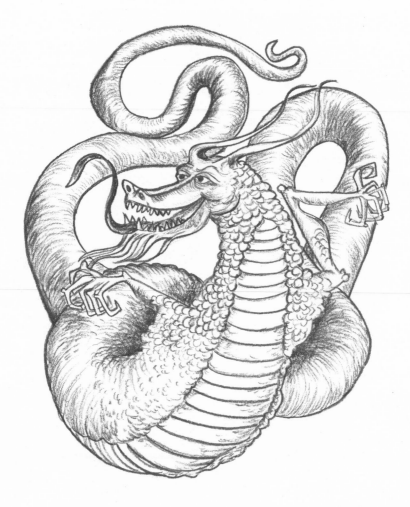

A LISTING OF THE DRAGON'S TALES